I0829051

Copyright 2026 Shield of Faith Press
Translation 2026 Juliana Staab on behalf of Shield of Faith Press
All rights reserved

ISBN: 978-1-967697-02-1

Direct inquiries to:
Shield of Faith Press, an AMDG Company
8399 Melrose Drive
Overland Park, KS 66214
The United States of America

The Blessed Carmelite Martyrs of Compiègne

Translation of "*Les Bienheureuses Carmélites de Compiègne,*" by Victor Pierre. Fourth Edition, Victor Lecoffre, 1906.

Victor Pierre

Nihil obstat

Romae, 15 *Decembris* 1904

ANGELUS ADV. MARIANI

S.R.C. Assessor

Imprimatur

Parisiis, die 19 *Decembris* 1904

P. FAGES

V. g.

AUTHOR's DECLARATION

By using in this book terms such as Saints, Martyrs, Blessed, or miracles in reference to the servants of God who have not yet been raised to the altar, the author intends to do so only in the sense and to the extent of the decrees of Urban VIII dated March 13, 1625, and June 4, 1631, and in no way wishes to anticipate the judgment of the Church, to whose authority he respectfully submits.

—Victor Pierre, Paris, November 4, 1904.

TABLE OF CONTENTS

FORMER EDITOR's NOTE

It is with a particularly lively emotion that we offer to the public this new volume in our collection. The author had barely finished correcting his final drafts when he was taken from his family and friends in a matter of seconds. A sudden death is not necessarily an "unexpected" death for a Christian with clear faith, firm common sense, and faithful religious practice, as Victor Pierre had always been. We are confident, moreover, that the holy Carmelites, of whom he thought constantly in the last hours of his life, will have eased his sudden passing by covering him with their efficacious protection. Mr. Victor Pierre was both a man of science and a man of action, devoting all of his free time to the defense and propagation of the Truth. We expected additional works from him, notably on the history of the Revolution, which he had studied in depth. However, we admit that he could not have ended his career better than by bequeathing to his widow and numerous children this last souvenir of his Catholic zeal and his thorough scholarship. We therefore hope that no reader of this beautiful book will refuse to pray for the repose — the well-earned repose — of his soul.

— Henri Joly.

PREFACE

On July 17, 1794, sixteen Carmelite Nuns from the monastery of Compiègne appeared before the Revolutionary Tribunal of Paris and, condemned to death as *fanatics,* together mounted the scaffold erected in the *Place du Trône*[1] that same day.

By a decree dated December 16, 1902, Pope Leo XIII declared them Venerable; a second decree, which we hope will be made very soon, will declare them Martyrs[2]. This is the first time that, among the victims of the Terror, the Church has chosen to raise some of them to the altar.

The canonical investigations She institutes for this purpose are based on the most authentic documents, and it can be said that, through the choice of witnesses and the independence She assures them, as well as through the rigorous and patient thoroughness with which documents and depositions are examined from both sides in Rome, these trials, which seem to have no other purpose than to establish the fact of martyrdom, also provide history with as many resources as guarantees.

I have not neglected to study these processes, and I have gleaned from them many insights, but I have relied mainly on the original documents. Before embarking on the narrative, I do not think it irrelevant to make them known to the reader.

***

There three especially important documents: in chronological order, they are the *Memoirs* of Monsieur Jauffret,[3] published in 1803; *Les Martyrs de la Foi* (The Martyrs of the Faith), that Abbé Guillon published in 1821; and finally, the account of one of the Carmelite Nuns of Compiègne who had escaped

1 [TN] The "Throne Square". Also known as the *Place de la Nation,* or the *Place du Trône-Renversé.*

2 They were declared Martyrs and Blessed on May 27, 1906.

3 [EN] Gaspard-André Jauffret (1759-1823), Catholic priest and later bishop of Metz and Aix-en-Provence. – "*Monsieur*" (literally "my lord") is used as an honorary title for nobles or priests in the *Ancien régime* context.

the fate of her companions: her writings did not appear until 1836, after her death. But in order to understand the relationship between these three documents, it is necessary to **reverse the dates** and speak first about Sister Marie of the Incarnation: although outwardly her testimony came last, she was nonetheless the inspiration for the first two.

***

First, may the reader kindly permit me to defer the following until Chapter 2 of this book[4]: the mysterious birth of Françoise-Geneviève Philippe, known in religion as Sister Josephine-Marie of the Incarnation; her former state of illness; her miraculous healing in Pontoise before the tomb of Madame Acarie;[5] and her vocation to Carmel.

For seven years and seven months, from September 23, 1786, to the first days of May 1794, she was an eyewitness of what happened at the Carmelite convent in Compiègne, both in the monastery and during the period of their dispersion. In May 1794, personal affairs called her to Paris, and detained her there, where she met with the Mother Prioress. Her conversation with her on June 21 marked the end of her relationship with the Carmel of Compiègne: from that moment on, her accounts are based solely on hearsay.

In March 1795, eight months after the execution of her Sisters, we find her in Compiègne, where she made contact with the English Benedictine Nuns. From there, she retired to Orléans, where she spent several years; according to Monsieur Jauffret, she was still there in 1803. It was in Orléans that she met Denis Blot, a vinedresser who, while imprisoned in the *Conciergerie*[6], had met the Carmelites and rendered

4 In this preface, I am obliged to refer to many circumstances that the reader will only learn about through the book: I had to come to terms with this inconvenience in order to avoid endless explanations and repetitions.

5 [EN] Blessed Marie of the Incarnation (1566-1618), best known as Madame Acarie, founder of the Discalded Carmel in France.

6 [TN] The *Conciergerie* (English: Lodge) is a former courthouse and

them some services. He escaped the Revolutionary Tribunal. One month after 9 Thermidor, a decree of the Committee of Public Safety and General Security restored his freedom[7]. He was convinced that he owed his release to the prayers of the holy Nuns of Compiègne. "That is what he told me," recounted Sister Marie of the Incarnation, "when I myself, led by Providence to Orléans in month of October 1795, saw this brave man, whose first impulse was to throw himself around my neck, saying, 'I had the good fortune to know all of your holy ladies, etc.'"

From 1803 to 1823, we lose track of Madame Philippe, as she no longer used her religious name. About twenty Carmels had been reestablished, but she did not enter any of them; if for no other reason, her poor health would have prevented her from doing so. Did she live in Paris? It seems so, and that from time to time she saw Mother Raphaël, a former Nun from the monastery of Saint-Denis who was trying to rebuild a community on *Rue Cassini,* near the *Observatoire.* There she met Mother Euphrasie Binart, who had just founded a convent of the Order of Notre-Dame in the *Maison des oiseaux;* Angélique Fouchet, later Mother Joseph in religion, a pupil of Mother Euphrasie[8]; and Mother Émilienne, sister of Anne Pelras, from Compiègne. From these individuals, who had lived in Paris during the Revolution, and who had been within the Catholic circles, she was able to gather some information.

---

prison in Paris located on the west of the *Île de la Cité* below the *Palais de Justice.* It was originally part of the former royal palace, the *Palais de la Cité,* which also included the *Sainte-Chapelle.* Two large medieval halls remain from the royal palace. During the French Revolution, 2,781 prisoners, including Marie Antoinette, were imprisoned, tried and sentenced at the *Conciergerie* then sent to different sites to be executed by the guillotine. It is now a national monument and museum.

7 Archives of the Prefecture of Police, Box 23, no. 612. The decree (10 Fructidor Year II) is signed by Goupilleau, Barbeau-Dubarran, Louis (from Bas-Rhin), Dumont, Philippe Rühl, and Legendre.

8 She wrote somewhere: "I know this from an eyewitness, Angélique Fouchet."

On September 23, 1823, Madame Philippe joined the Carmelites of Sens, but as a boarder; she could not have endured the penitent and mortified life of a Nun. She remained there for thirteen years and died on January 10, 1836, in her seventy-fifth year.

For four years, her director had been Monsieur Villecourt, Vicar General of Sens and superior of the Carmel in that city. He encouraged her to write about the events of her life, but her humility prevented her from agreeing. He then urged her to recount what she knew about her companions; this account was not intended for the public, but was to be included as a part of the *Chronicles* of the Order reserved for the house of Compiègne. Out of obedience, she agreed. Monsieur Villecourt, who was very absorbed in his duties, did not press her: it even seems that after making this suggestion, he no longer discussed the project further with her, and personally forgot about it. It was only upon the death of the former Carmelite that, charged by his capacity as superior of the house with sorting through her papers, he found a certain number of loose sheets of paper on which she had attempted, at least partially, to respond to the desire of her director.

What a happy discovery! "God," he said, "had His reasons for snatching her from the death that had reaped her illustrious companions. He preserved her so that we might learn about the virtues, sufferings, struggles, and victories of that holy company to which she had belonged. What a loss to the history of that era if we had been deprived of such edifying details!"

Monsieur Villecourt was right; but before examining her account and its publication, we must ask ourselves whether it was the first one written by Sister Marie of the Incarnation, or whether, long before that, she had drawn up at least two others, which were, directly or indirectly, communicated to Monsieur Jauffret and Abbé Guillon and which served as the framework for their own accounts.

***

In 1803, Monsieur Jauffret, then Vicar General to Cardinal Fesch, Archbishop of Lyon, and who in 1806 would become Bishop of Metz, published two volumes in-8° with Le Clere, the printer of the Archdiocese of Paris, under the title: *Mémoires pour servir à l'histoire de la Religion à la fin du XVIIIe siècle*[9]. He did not sign them: this was prudence. He had collected the episodes of the religious persecution: the rulers of that time preferred that one should keep quiet about them. In Volume II, page 351, one finds the *Relation de la fin glorieuse des religieuses carmélites de Compiègne condamnées à mort par le Tribunal révolutionnaire de Paris le 17 juillet 1794*[10].

At the bottom of the first page, we read this note: "We are writing this account based on the handwritten testimony of eight trustworthy individuals; we have also consulted, or had consulted, several Carmelite Nuns who knew those of Compiègne, and who were able to certify the same facts. One of these Nuns had been a Professed member of this latter house" (p. 351). At the end of his account, speaking of three Nuns of Compiègne who survived, he quotes Sister Marie of the Incarnation, "now known as Madame Philippe, currently in Orléans, one of the witnesses whom we have consulted for the writing of this article" (p. 371).

His avowal is not disguised. He "had her consulted": she replied, obviously in writing. However, in comparing the text of Monsieur Jauffret with that of the Carmelite, it is easy to notice, by the consistency of the facts, details, and even sentences, that he borrowed heavily from her, or rather, that his numerous borrowings formed the bulk of his own account. Thus, he is indebted to her writings for: 1. The details about the English Benedictines (p. 352); 2. The scene on Rue Saint-Antoine, when the carts passed by (p. 356); 3. Everything

9 [TN] *Memoirs for the History of Religion at the End of the 18th Century*

10 [TN] *Account of the Glorious End of the Carmelite Nuns of Compiègne who were Condemned to Death by the Revolutionary Tribunal of Paris on July 17, 1794*

relating to Sir Blot, whom the Sister had met in Orléans; 4. The hymn is set to the tune of *La Marseillaise*, which he analyzes with exactitude, verse by verse, without quoting the lyrics; 5. The account of the hearing of the Revolutionary Tribunal; 6. That of the execution; and finally 7. The list of the Nuns with their ages, the date of their Profession, and a final note about the three Sisters who escaped the scaffold.

Monsieur Jauffret mentions seven other people who were "trustworthy." He does not name them; they were undoubtedly trustworthy, but inaccurately informed, and they caused him to make a few mistakes. According to him (p. 352), the Carmelites were arrested "around the first days of May 1794," whereas they were arrested on June 22nd, a month and a half later. He adds: "The stay of the Carmelites in this prison (at the Visitation) lasted barely a month." It was exactly twenty-one days (June 22-July 12). "They were taken to Paris on June 10th or 11th." It was on July 12th that they left Compiègne; they arrived in Paris on the 13th. Finally, he has them spend thirty-five days at the Conciergerie, when in fact they spent only five days there (July 18-17).

From the borrowings made by Monsieur Jauffret, it is easy to notice what was contained in the first manuscript of Sister Marie of the Incarnation, and also what was not contained in it: as it stood, it was already rich in information.

***

In 1800, Abbé Guillon announced in his newspaper, *La politique chrétienne* (Christian Politics), the forthcoming publication of his work, *Les Martyrs de la Foi pendant la Révolution française*[11], for which he had been gathering material since 1797. Fouché, the Minister of the General Police, concerned about the impact these unearthings of revolutionary crimes might have, and thinking he was responding to the intentions of the First Consul, had the papers of Abbé Guillon seized by his officers. In 1814, these papers were found at the Prefecture

11 [TN] *The Martyrs of the Faith during the French Revolution*

of the Police[12]. The author then continued his work and published it in 1821. The first volume contains a preliminary discourse whose theories on the conditions of martyrdom have provoked just criticisms. The remaining three volumes are a compilation of notes in alphabetical order about all of those – male or female, laymen or ecclesiastics, religious or secular – who were victims of the so-called revolutionary justice.

Undoubtedly, he was familiar with the *Relation* of Monsieur Jauffret, but he added a great deal to it. Devoting a personal entry for each of the sixteen Nuns, he was forced to find some personal details about each of them. He did not fail to do so, but since he did not find these in the work of Monsieur Jauffret, he had to look elsewhere.

Three Carmelites from Compiègne had escaped execution; at least two were still alive. It does not seem that Abbé Guillon knew them; indeed, in the article on Madame Brard (**v.** II, p. 305), we read: "If, of the three Nuns from the same community in Compiègne who, not being found with their Sisters when they were arrested, and thus escaped death – namely: Sister Saint Stanislas, Sister Thérèse of Jesus, and the Sister of the Immaculate Conception (by which he means to say Sister Marie of the Incarnation) – if any of them are still living, she will attest to the truth of what we have said, and what we will say elsewhere, about their martyred Sisters."

But since Abbé Guillon had no personal connections with these Nuns, nor even with the third, does it follow that he did not have before his eyes a manuscript by one of them, and by the only one who could have informed him, namely, Sister Marie of the Incarnation? Between the *Relation,* printed later, and the notes of Abbé Guillon, the similarities are so numerous and so striking that it must have been that Abbé

12 [TN] Headed by the Prefect of Police, it is an agency of the Government of France under the administration of the Ministry of the Interior. Part of the National Police, it provides a police force for an area limited by department borders. It was formed in 1800.

Guillon had either known of and virtually copied a manuscript by Sister Marie of the Incarnation, or she must have copied Abbé Guillon.

This second hypothesis is not likely. How could Abbé Guillon have known about the character or lives of Madames Lidoine, Brard, de Croissy, Chrétien, Thouret, and Pelras, which he emphasizes more than the others, if someone who had lived with them had not informed him? And who else could have done so but Sister Marie of the Incarnation? She had not seen him, they did not know each other; but, at that time, there must have been a manuscript of hers prior to the one that was later published, distinct from the one known to Monsieur Jauffret, and which some intermediary must have communicated to Abbé Guillon. The confidence with which he defies contradiction suggests that he had in his hands indisputable evidence.

One may, however, note a few differences. For example, in the scene depicting the oath of liberty and equality, Abbé Guillon either did not know or did not want to follow the account of Sister Marie of the Incarnation. But this is a difference of interpretation than a difference of text. Similarly, there are things that he either ignores, or which the manuscript of the Sister was less detailed at the time than it later became. For example, regarding Madame Chrétien, he seems to know only her marriage, but nothing about the circumstances that preceded her entry into religion. On the contrary, the account of the audience is remarkably similar to that of the Sister's, and, as in her account, the questions and answers are quoted directly. There is no doubt that in this part, one of the two writers copied the other. There are places where the sentences of the Abbé and those of the Sister are repeated in identical terms — *Martyrs de la Foi* (*Martyrs of the Faith*), Lidoine, v. III, p. 569; Pelras, **v.** IV, p. 220, etc.

***

Let us return to Sister Marie of the Incarnation. Based on

observations suggested by our examination of the *Relation* of Monsieur Jauffret and of the notes of Abbé Guillon, it seems to us that before 1803, she wrote a first draft, from which she excluded the details relating to each Nun in order to focus on the general facts; that later, she wrote a second draft, consisting entirely of notes, which in this way corresponded to the plan of the book of Abbé Guillon, who also had the work of Monsieur Jauffret at his disposal. The manuscript we have yet to discuss is less a new work than a third draft of the two previous ones with a few additions.

On the first page, we read: *Relation de la mort des Carmélites de Compiègne*[13]. Then, immediately after, and in the midst of some erasures: "If I wanted to undertake to report in detail the acts of virtue which I had seen them practice during the seven and a half years that I had the good fortune to live in the company of my Mothers and Sisters in Compiègne, there would be enough to fill several volumes; but since God has seen fit to deny me the talent necessary to accomplish this task, I will give only simple excerpts from the life and death of each of them." And immediately, we read: "First, the Reverend Mother Marie-Thérèse of Saint Augustine, etc." Followed by the other Nuns: first, the Professed, then, the Novice and the three Converse[14] Sisters, and finally, the two Extern Sisters.

Another manuscript begins in the middle of a sentence, as a fragment detached from the whole. It contains details about Blot, the vinedresser; the verses of the hymn that the Sisters composed at the *Conciergerie*; the circumstances surrounding the performance and retraction of the oath of liberty and equality; and anecdotes, some of which are repeated from the first part.

A third manuscript contains, here and there, a few pages or a few lines that are not found in the other two.[15]

13 [TN] *Account of the Death of the Carmelites of Compiègne*

14 [TN] Also called Lay Sisters.

15 In 1891, the Carmel of Sens gave these manuscripts to the Carmel of

In addition, there were many documents that, as a precaution during the Revolution of 1848, the Carmel of Sens entrusted to various individuals, but which were not returned to them.

Monsieur Villecourt could have limited himself to reproducing the first manuscript, which forms a homogeneous and coherent whole, and used the surplus to compose an interesting appendix in which he could have provided the order that was lacking in this part of the original. He preferred to give the publication a style that he considered more literary and, for readers, more enjoyable. He broke with the plan of the author and divided her short and modest pages into three books, each divided into chapters. The first book, devoted to the general events that affected the Carmelites from 1790 until their death in 1794, is composed of excerpts from the individual accounts. The second reproduces these accounts. The third is a fictitious collection of various documents, some of which were found among the papers of Sister Marie of the Incarnation: letters from the Mother Prioress to Mademoiselle de Grand-Rut; a letter regarding the death of Bp. de la Motte, Bishop of Amiens; a letter from Reverend Mother Henriette of Jesus; a summary of the notice of Monsieur Rigaud, Superior; excerpts from *Le Moniteur*[16] of 1790 on the suppression of religious orders. He does not refrain from making a few omissions, either of pages or sentences, for reasons of convenience, nor from additions that are perhaps only the

---

Compiègne, as their rightful owner. I was able to see and consult them. The trial of the Ordinary, vol. II, provides a very accurate and detailed copy that is equivalent to a facsimile. A fourth manuscript, containing only anecdotes relating to the period prior to 1789, remained in the possession of the Carmel of Sens.

16 [TN] *Le Moniteur Universel* was a French newspaper founded in Paris on November 24, 1789, under the title *Gazette Nationale ou Le Moniteur Universel* by Charles-Joseph Panckoucke, and which ceased publication on December 31, 1868. It was the main French newspaper during the French Revolution and was for a long time the official journal of the French government and at times a propaganda publication, especially under the Napoleonic regime. *Le Moniteur* had a large circulation in France and Europe, and also in America during the French Revolution.

reproduction of fragments that are lost today, nor, in the text itself, from fairly minor but frequent changes of wording. It must be acknowledged that this loose reproduction in no way detracts from the authority and value of the document.[17]

Despite his duties as Vicar General of Sens, and despite his concerns as Bishop-Elect of La Rochelle, he pressed ahead with completing his work and published it in Sens in September 1836[18], the same year of the death of the Carmelite. It was a small 228-page book in-12 format, under the title: *Histoire des Religieuses carmélites de Compiègne, conduites à l'échafaud le 17 juillet 1794*[19]; a posthumous work by Sister Marie of the Incarnation, a Carmelite from the same monastery. Epigraph: *Infirma mundi elegit Deus ut confundat fortia*: God chose the weakest to confound the strongest; First Epistle to the Corinthians, Ch. II, v. 27, Sens, Published by Thomas-Malvin, printer and bookseller, 1836. Nowhere does the name of Monsieur Villecourt appear; but, one may guess that he is the Superior of the Carmel of Sens.

The Preface, which is very distinguished and deserves not to be separated from the book, is almost entirely devoted to Sister Marie of the Incarnation: "As we had the most intimate correspondence with her for four years, we can attest to the soundness of her judgment, which gave nothing to pure imagination and which, moreover, had no inclination toward vain credulity. The tenacity of her memory, which forgot nothing and in which everything was classified in order; the penetration of her mind, which never missed the slightest interesting detail; her truthfulness, which would not have allowed her to present as certain any fact that seemed doubtful to her; and her scrupulous attention to concealing

17 The numerous citations that I will make from Sister Marie of the Incarnation are entirely and exclusively taken from the original manuscript.

18 *Journal de la librairie*, no. 40. Saturday, October 1, 1836, no. 4901, in-12, nine and a half sheets.

19 [TN] *The History of the Carmelite Nuns of Compiègne, led to the scaffold on July 17, 1794*

neither the faults nor the good qualities of the people she speaks about, are so many reasons why we should accept her account with complete confidence, even if we had no other guarantee of her sincerity from the faith that animated her and in her status as a Nun.» (Preface, pp. 18-19). "I gathered together," he writes further on, «the scattered sheets that she did not have the time to arrange; I faithfully and scrupulously extracted from them the facts and words relating to this or that subject, putting them in the order and sequence that she certainly would have put them in had death not prevented her from doing so...The manuscript of the author, which is preserved in its entirety at the monastery of the Carmelites of Sens, is a lasting monument to the fidelity of my work." (pp. 28-29)[20]

Although there are some reservations to be made about the editing process followed by Monsieur Villecourt (and this process was not without notable precedents), we must thank him for the service he rendered to the cause of the Carmelites of Compiègne by publishing this testimony from such an important witness and by publishing it so promptly. Who knows whether, as a result of delays that could have been prolonged, this manuscript might not have suffered the same fate as those that have been lost! The account of Monsieur Jauffret and the notes of Abbé Guillon would have undoubtedly survived, but they would have been deprived of the added authority given to them by the authentic and irrefutable testimony of she who had guided and inspired them.

***

This moving and most-valuable account delighted a few Carmels but did not reach the general public. Ten years later (1845), Fr. Van der Moere, a Bollandist, borrowed material from it for a few enthusiastic columns in the *Gloria posthuma*

20 Monsieur Villecourt occupied the seat of La Rochelle from 1836 to 1856. In 1855, he was appointed Cardinal, resigned from his bishopric, and was called to Rome as Cardinal of the Curia, where he died in 1867.

Sanctœ Theresiœ.[21] On the other hand, two Catholic historians, Rohrbacher and Jager, do not seem to have been aware of the short work of Sister Marie of the Incarnation: they stuck to the account of Monsieur Jauffret, including the errors. It is surprising that Ludovic Sciout, who was so well informed about the facts of the religious persecution, omitted the Carmelites of Compiègne from his *Histoire de la Constitution civile du clergé*[22]. Emile Campardon, in both editions (1862 and 1867) of his *Histoire du tribunal révolutionnaire de Paris*[23], does not mention them either. Thiers, Louis Blanc, and Michelet are equally silent on the subject. It is to Alexandre Sorel, a former lawyer at the Paris Bar and president of the Civil Tribunal of Compiègne, that we owe, after Monsieurs Jauffret and Guillon, and Sr. Marie of the Incarnation, the first and only original work on the subject of the Carmelites.[24]

Sorel, who lived in Compiègne and was the author of notable monographs on *Le Couvent des Carmes pendant la Terreur*[25], on *Stanislas Maillard,* one of the organizers of the massacres of September 2nd, and on *Le Château de Chantilly pendant la Révolution*[26], was naturally tempted to apply his conscientious

21 [TN] *The Posthumous Glory of St. Teresa [of Avila]*

22 [TN] *The History of the Civil Constitution of the Clergy*

23 [TN] *The History of the Revolutionary Tribunal of Paris*

24 The Carmelites of Compiègne before the Revolutionary Tribunal (July 17, 1794). Account of their arrest, trial, and condemnation to death based on authentic and entirely unpublished documents with facsimiles, by *Alexandre* Sorel, member of the Historical Society of Compiègne, with the epigraph: *Semper et ubique veritas,* 1878. This work, first published in the *Bulletin de la Société historique de Compiègne* (The Bulletin of the Historical Society of Compiègne), of which Sorel was a member, was printed in a limited edition of only 150 copies and was hardly available in stores; this was insufficient publicity for a study whose interest extended beyond the city and the region. Despite his poor health, Sorel was able to testify at the trial of the Ordinary. He died in La Bosse, in the canton of Coudray-Saint-Germer (Oise), on August 28th, 1901, at the age of 75, as a faithful Catholic.

25 [TN] *The Convent of Carmel during the Terror*

26 [TN] *The Castle of Chantilly during the Revolution*

use of official documents and his precise scholarship to this local event. He was the first to consult the National Archives and those of the Oise department; in Compiègne, his duties as president of the court facilitated his research. It is the documentary evidence that makes his publication particularly valuable; sympathetic in his heart of hearts, in order to appear more independent, he affects to be neutral and not to be moved by the religious interest of the cause. However, undoubtedly won over by his subject, Sorel ended his book with the following lines, almost unexpected from his pen: "Nearly a century has passed since the sinister executions which we have just recalled. Victims and executioners now belong to history. But God has already determined the fate of each. To some, the palms of martyrdom, the glory of Heaven, a good example on earth, and the admiration of successive generations; to others, the shame and contempt of all humanity." (p. 92) It seemed to us that it was not without a certain pride that Sorel, before the Ecclesiastical Tribunal, and enlightened by age and by the success of a cause to which he felt his book was no stranger, recounted the lines we have just quoted.

***

Even with these various and useful documents, even with the depositions contained in the canonical trials, among which it would be unfair not to mention those of the Carmelites of Paris, Sens, and Compiègne and the English Benedictines of Stanbrook, as well as the highly competent and well-informed study supplied by Father Ory of the Society of Jesus, there remain more than a few problems, albeit secondary ones, on which opinions are divided. After long and careful reflection, in all sincerity, I too have come up with a solution: the reader will judge.

Victor PIERRE

Mantes-la-Ville (Seine-et-Oise),

September 19, 1904

THE SIXTEEN CARMELITES OF COMPIEGNE

CHAPTER I

THE MONASTERY OF THE ANNUNCIATION OF THE CARMELITES OF COMPIÈGNE (1641-1789)

To the left of the Castle of Compiègne, on the site now occupied by the Castle Theater and a cavalry barracks, between *Rue Osthenin* and *Rue du Four*, there was, at the time of the Revolution, a convent of Carmelites with a chapel, outbuildings, and gardens. It was the fifty-third convent of its Order founded in France. Six Nuns from Amiens and two from Paris, arrived in 1641 and first lived on *Rue des Minimes* at the *Hôtel de la Toison d'Or*. Then, for four years, they lived in the left wing of the castle; and thirdly, at the *Hôtel de Toulouse*. During this time, their numbers had grown, and thanks to the resources they had acquired, they were able to purchase a plot of land and build their own residence there. The first visitors and superiors had already given the nascent monastery the name of the Monastery of the Annunciation. The day before the eve of this feast, March 23rd, 1647, the Carmelites moved in.

The favor granted to them by Anne of Austria, then Queen regent, in giving them asylum at the castle, was only the beginning of many other favors, such as the relationships that were immediately established with the royal family and which continued from reign to reign. Anne of Austria brought Louis XIV there as a child, bearing rich gifts for the chapel.

Maria Theresa visited there frequently when the Court was in Compiègne.[1] Louis XIV visited with his brother, with his nephew the Duke of Chartres, and also with his grandsons. He inquired with interest about the Nuns who had known his mother. When Maria Theresa died he told the Carmelites: "She is a saint; pray for her and for my entire household." He loved them for their regularity, their poverty, their hidden life, and their content with a small house, instead of dreaming of building in the fashion of so many others. Reporting these praises to the Mother Prioress, Madame de Maintenon[2] added: "I heard these words with great joy, loving you always tenderly. So redouble your prayers for the King, and never tire of asking for peace."

The generosity of princes, and of the Count of Toulouse in particular, prompted the community to erect a chapel more worthy of the guests it received. Marie Leczinska[3] also contributed to this project with her personal funds and gifts. During the long stays of the Court in Compiègne, the Queen often visited the monastery, spending several days there on retreat and loving to spend hours there with her daughters. On ceremonial days, her daughters enjoyed serving as readers, or even as servers, in the refectory[4]. On these occasions,

1 [EN] Compiègne has been a royal residence of the French kings since the early middle ages. They especially enjoyed the massive Compiègne forest for hunting.

2 [EN] Louis XIV's second wife.

3 [EN] Queen of France as the wife of Louis XV, between 1725 and 1768.

4 [TN] In Carmel, during the main meal (Lunch, but in the monastery called "Dinner"), and the evening meal (called "Supper", or on fast days, "Collation"), there is always a Sister assigned for the week to be the reader at the meal. There is a special place in the refectory set up for her to sit and read from a book of spiritual reading – so that as the body is being nourished, the soul is also. Additionally, each week a different Sister is given the duty of being the "server" in the refectory for these two meals. This means that as the reading is being done, the server is serving the food and drink to each Sister in turn, beginning with the Reverend Mother. Instead of helping herself to food when she is finished, she remains ready to serve even second portions to her Sisters during the entire mealtime. This

to be more at ease, they would take off their court dresses and change into other, very simple ones that they had had made for this purpose and which remained inside the house. During morning recreation, the Queen spun wool in order to, as she said, make tunics for her dear Carmelites. She liked the ceremonies of the Taking of the Habit and of the Veil[5] to be postponed until the Court came to Compiègne, and she never failed to attend with her daughters, often giving the veil herself.

These long and frequent visits to the Carmelites of Compiègne had sustained Madame Louise[6] in her religious vocation and in her choice of Carmel. While the Mothers of Rue de Grenelle taught her the Constitutions of Saint Teresa, it was with those of Compiègne that she studied the austerities of the Rule. The day after a ceremony of the Taking the Habit, she wrote to the Prioress: "I have a favor to ask of you, but in the strictest confidence, so that no one else knows: I would like you to send me the serge tunic that your Novice wore yesterday when she took the habit.... You can send it to me

---

gives the opportunity for the Nuns to take turns in serving Christ in the persons of their Sisters, and of fulfilling what our Lord said regarding the corporeal works of mercy: *"I was hungry, and you gave Me to eat....Thirsty and you gave Me to drink....You did it to Me."*

5 [TN] These are two distinct ceremonies. The ceremony of the Taking of the Habit is when a Postulant becomes a Novice, and she receives the habit of the Order as well as her new religious name. Depending on the customs of the community, she may wear a wedding dress at the beginning of this ceremony; and, before she receives the habit and veil of a Novice, her hair – symbol and treasure of her feminine beauty – will be cut. The Ceremony of the Taking of the Veil is when the Novice professes vows, and thus receives the veil of a Professed religious, namely, the black veil – signifying her complete death to the world.

6 [EN] Louise de France (1737-1787), youngest daughter of Louis XV. She became a Carmelite nun in 1770, and was declared Venerable by the Church in 1873. Her prayers and sacrifices certainly helped her father Louis XV, who led an extremely debauched and scandalous life, to eventually repent from his sins on his deathbed.

one morning through your Extern[7], wrapped in a well-sealed envelope, with instructions that the package be given to me personally." Later, when she was at the Carmel of Saint-Denis[8], she wrote again to the Prioress of Compiègne: "I owe you many apologies for all the tricks I played on you to learn all the details of your holy practices, not to mention the tunic I robbed from you. Now, you know where my questions came from, and surely you have forgiven me everything..."[9] At Saint-Denis, she was reunited with Mother of the Child Jesus as her Novice Mistress, and whom she had known as Prioress in Compiègne. It was to this Carmel that her preferences would have led her, but the King formally opposed it: "Compiègne is not possible," he wrote her. Wouldn't the austerities of a princess of France in Carmel not be too much in comparison to the life of pleasure led at the castle? Nevertheless, the royal Carmelite maintained her relationship with the monastery throughout her life; she sent her subjects there and even

---

7 [TN] An Extern (Sister) was in charge of taking care of the duties on the outside of the monastery. She did not live inside with the other cloistered Nuns, and thus was not bound to enclosure. Examples of her duties would be: cleaning the non-cloistered part of the chapel, meeting guests, receiving certain donations given from the outside, going on errands, tending to the non-cloistered gardens, etc.

8 [TN] This Carmel was in Paris, just north of Montmartre, close to the Cathedral of Saint-Denis. The convent's first stone was laid in 1628 by Marie de Medicis. The Carmel became famous due to Madame Louise's entrance, being the daughter of Louis XV. She was first a simple Nun, later becoming Mother Superior. On her instigation, the Carmel was given a new chapel designed by Richard Mique, architect to the King. Louis XV often visited his daughter and a private house for him was built on the convent's southeast corner. After the French Revolution, these Carmelites disbanded. The building was turned into a barracks, and the garden, which had become the property of the Republic, was rented out. It was acquired by Descemet, the Parisian nurseryman. In 1803, his catalogue listed 52 varieties of apple tree, 58 of plum trees and 115 of pear trees.

9 *Vie de la R. Mère Thérèse de Saint-Augustin, Madame Louise de France*, par une religieuse de sa communauté (The Life of the Reverend Mother Therese of Saint Augustine, Madame Louis de France, by a Nun of her community), v. I, p. 72-73 et 154.

reserved for it novices whose more substantial dowries[10] could bring some relief to this poor community. She obtained from Marie-Antoinette that she could pay for the dowry of Madame Lidoine from her own personal funds. During the years of trial, Madame Lidoine would later become the Prioress of the monastery.

A second characteristic of the monastery of Compiègne was its regularity. Several documents bear witness to this: first, from 1720 to 1791, the collection of circulars that were customarily sent to the monasteries of the Order on the occasion of the death of their Nuns: those from Compiègne are particularly edifying. The reports of the visitors are no less favorable. In 1789, these visitors were Monsieur Rigaud, his two nephews, Messers. de Brassac and Juge de Brassac, and Monsieur de Floirac, the latter being Vicar General of Paris. Their letters, preserved in the Archives, are remarkable for the temperance they bring to the ardor of mortification that animated the Nuns. During his visit in 1780, Monsieur Rigaud congratulated them on their perfect regularity; he did not judge it opportune to add new regulations to those he had previously established, as the former had been strictly observed. He noted a healthy competition among the Sisters in the diligence shown in their community exercises, at prayer, and during the Divine Office. On the subject of silence, which he called "one of the most essential points of the Constitutions," he said, "I am pleased to see that you are making this the particular object of your attention and care: you are all striving to be the most faithful." He praised them no less for their love of poverty: "You know, my daughters, the terrible examples that I have mentioned to you of the consequences of such attachments which Nuns have even for trifles. But," he added fondly, "it would be useless to say more on this subject, and I really do not know which point to emphasize. I am like those people who are searching,

10 [EN] The family of the nun would provide a dowry to the monastery, just as they would provide a dowry for a daughter who is getting married.

searching always when they are in confession because they have nothing to say. It was necessary that I search well for a long time to be able to say a few words to you."

To these touching testimonies, another is added, one that is very valuable for the period. Jansenism had crept into some Carmels, particularly around 1737; the monastery of Saint-Denis had been the most seriously affected by it. During her time as Prioress, Madame Louise de France welcomed with eager charity one of the Mothers of this monastery, aged 91, who, weary of heresy, nevertheless hesitated to ask to return to the monastery. The monastery of Compiègne had escaped these errors: "The Jansenist heresy," said some circulars, "never approached this house." At the height of its popularity, each time a Sister died, care was taken to note the name of the confessor who had assisted her. Most often it was a Jesuit, and mention was made of the Catholic profession of faith she had made before her death to testify to her union with the Roman Church.

Among the events which were warning signs of a revolution announced by the philosophers, and whose lamentable excesses were denounced by the sacred orators, such as Father Beauregard and Father Ch. Frey de Neuville, with details that had the precision of prophecy, there was one that related more directly to the Order of Carmelites: I am referring to the edicts of suppression issued by Emperor Joseph II against the convents of men and women scattered throughout his vast empire. The vigilant solicitude of Madame Louise de France had secured the consent of her nephew, the King [Louis XVI], to offer the Carmelites of the Netherlands asylum in the monasteries of France. She urged them to accept, fearing nothing more than seeing them disperse and renounce religious life. For their part, the Carmelites of Belgium[11] opposed the threats of revolution hanging over France and were in no hurry to make up their minds. The express command of Joseph II to finally enforce the edicts forced

11 [EN] Belgium was part of the Holy Roman Empire back then.

them to make a decision. All the trials and tribulations that our Nuns in France would soon have to endure were already familiar to those in Belgium: raids by the administrative authorities, inventories of movable and immovable property, seizures and sales, administrative interventions in internal affairs. All the details of this base persecution must have reached the attention of our Carmelites and struck even the most far-sighted among them as a preview of the trials which would, soon, affect them also.

The Carmelites of Brussels, Dendermonde, Vilvoorde, Aalst, Bruges, and Tournai decided to go to France: Madame Louise of France facilitated their journey. All of them first came to Saint-Denis; some, like those from Brussels and Aalst, to stay there and take their place in the Community; others to accept the hospitality of the convents on the *Rue d'Enfer, Rue de Grenelle, Rue Chapon*, or other convents. This was in June 1783. The Carmel of Compiègne, which was on the route of these exiles, had prepared a reception for them; but, eager to reach their destination, the Nuns from Brussels accepted only a "refreshment," overwhelmed as they were by the marks of affection shown to them by their French Sisters. Only one of these Nuns, Sister Caroline from the monastery of Vilvoorde, remained in Compiègne: she stayed there for seven years, until the death of Joseph II reopened the doors of her country to her and her Sisters, while new laws put an end to French hospitality.

These examples coming from abroad, could be seen as symptoms of the trials that the near future held in store for the Nuns of France. Our Carmelites of Compiègne prepared themselves for this without fear. There prevailed a tradition among them that an entire community would be called to martyrdom: with an ardor of hope that did not exclude humility, they dared to believe that this privilege would be reserved for them. This is a tribute that must be paid to the truth, however strange it may be to our overly human thoughts. We might be inclined to say: "Sinister destinies!"

Whereas, at the Carmel of Compiègne, they would have said: "Glorious!"

We will introduce each of these Carmelites to our readers one by one.

CHAPTER II

THE NUNS OF THE MONASTERY OF COMPIÈGNE IN 1789

In 1789, the Carmelite monastery of Compiègne had sixteen Choir Nuns, three Converse (or white veiled) Nuns, and one Novice. In addition to these twenty individuals, two Extern Sisters, non-religious, took care of the duties on the outside.[1]

The Prioress in charge at the time, Madeleine-Claudine Lidoine, was born in Paris on September 22, 1752, in the parish of Saint-Sulpice. At a young age, she had expressed her vocation for Carmel, but her family was too modest to be able to provide her with a dowry. She was introduced to Madame Louise de France, then Prioress of the Carmel of Saint-Denis. Impressed by the intelligence of this young girl, her precocious fervor, and the qualities she showed promise of developing, Madame Louise obtained permission from Marie-Antoinette, then Dauphine, to draw from her private funds the religious dowry of her protégée and sent her to the monastery of Compiègne.

She entered Carmel in August 1773, took the habit three months later, on November 14, the feast of All Saints of the Order, and made her profession on May 16th or 17th in 1775, six months longer than required for the novitiate; The profession may have been delayed to coincide with the visit of someone from the Court, Marie-Antoinette for example, who, having provided the dowry, may have wished to attend the

1 [TN] Choir Nuns made solemn vows, wore a black veil, and chanted the entire Divine Office each day. The Converse Sisters wore a white veil, did not pray either all or most of the Divine Office (substituting this with other vocal prayers), and took care of the greater part of the manual labors of the monastery (i.e. cooking, cleaning, gardening, laundry, etc). A Novice was a Nun who was in formation, and did not yet pronounce her vows. Extern Sisters were not technically Nuns, and lived on the outside of the enclosure, taking care of the exterior duties of the monastery.

ceremony. The new Professed took the name Thérèse of Saint Augustine: it was that of her august protector, the Prioress of Saint-Denis.

The careful education she had received and her natural qualities found their fulfillment in the cloister: her companions and ecclesiastical superiors quickly appreciated her religious virtues, her strength of character, and the benefits that the community could expect from her. In 1785, after only eleven years of profession, she was elected Prioress. She succeeded Mother Henriette of Jesus, whose wisdom and prudence were reflected in the new dignitary: "Very hard on herself," said Marie of the Incarnation, "and mortified to excess, her attention was entirely focused on the needs of the Sisters, having the secret of passing off the privations she imposed on herself as a matter of course." At the end of her three-year term, that is to say, in 1788, her election was renewed. For the difficult years that were to follow, she was entrusted with the leadership of the community. Her new duties would manifest even more vividly her energy, her courage, and her religious zeal, but let us not anticipate events.

The Sub-Prioress, Mother Saint-Louis, born Marie-Anne Brideau in Belfort on December 7, 1752, was two and a half months younger than the Mother Prioress, but three years her senior in the order of profession (September 3, 1771). Gentle, modest, and quiet, she was particularly devoted to maintaining the regularity of the Divine Office, the chant and the observance of the rubrics.

Mother Henriette of Jesus, in the world Marie-Françoise-Gabrielle de Croissy, grandniece of Colbert, born in Paris on June 18, 1745, was barely sixteen years old when Bp. de la Motte d'Orléans, the Bishop of Amiens, came in person to Compiègne to present her to the Carmel. The Prioress (who must have been Mother Catherine of Mercy, née Le Féron) objected on the grounds of her age and apparently fragile health. The prelate insisted: "Receive her, my Mother," he said, "receive her. I am certain of the consolation that she will give to the Community." The Prioress stood firm and postponed her admission for a year. When the delay expired, the young Postulant returned, was admitted (October 21, 1762), and on February 22, 1764, before reaching her nineteenth year, she made her Profession; but the Taking of the Veil[2] was postponed until the following July, Queen Marie Leczinska having desired to be present.

Entering the convent with youthful enthusiasm, her initial fervor, far from waning, grew stronger every day. "It seemed clear," said Sister Marie of the Incarnation, "that she was led to God by love, and it is true to say that she rendered herself even more admirable for the qualities of her heart, her tender piety, her zeal, and the happy assemblage of all the virtues of religion than for her natural talents and the knowledge she had acquired." She was elected Prioress at the age of thirty-four, in 1779. Re-elected at the end of her first three-year term, when the second term was over, the statutes prohibited her re-election for a third term, but she remained in office for another eighteen months since Bp. d'Argentré, Bishop of Sées, who was to preside over the vote, had to postpone his arrival. It was even assumed that these delays were not without intention: she was the only one to complain about them. From Prioress, she became Mistress of Novices. Her conduct was "a living rule" and her example reinforced all her counsels. "Her heart was to us the heart of a true mother." Her tenderness for her Novices was reciprocated, and in the

2 [TN] The ceremony of the Taking of the Veil in Carmel is distinct from the ceremony of Final Profession. For example, in St. Thérèse of Lisieux's case, on September 8, 1890 she made her Final Profession of vows in a private ceremony (which, usually would be done in the Chapter Room in the presence of one's Sisters alone). This ceremony would be preceded by some days of personal, silent retreat. But, it was not until September 24, 1890, that St. Thérèse underwent the beautiful ceremony of the Taking the Veil, when she would formally receive the black veil of a Professed Nun. This was a public ceremony in the main chapel, with any number of priests and faithful being permitted to attend. During this entire ceremony, the curtains and wooden-shutters covering the chapel's grille were opened, so that everyone on the outside of the Nun's choir could see it in its entirety.

letters of the Nuns preserved in the Archives, hardly is one found which does not contain a most affectionate memory of "the dear Mother Henriette."

Two Nuns, both born in 1715, were the doyennes of the community.

Anne Marie-Madeleine Thouret, known in religion as Sister Charlotte of the Resurrection, had entered Carmel following a ball where a tragic event, which is not specified, had inspired in her an absolute horror of life in the world.

She entered on March 18, 1736; she did not take her vows until August 19, 1740, more than four years later. This delay is noteworthy, given the Carmelite custom of not allowing the novitiate to continue beyond one year. Except for the office of Prioress, she held all the other offices: *tourière* of the inside turn[3], sacristan, treasurer, then twice, in 1764 and 1778, Sub-Prioress, and finally infirmarian. The devotion she showed in this last office was taken to the extreme; although her health was compromised, she asked as a favor not to be removed from it.[4]

Marie-Anne Piedcourt, Sister [Marie] of Jesus Crucified,

3 [TN] The cloistered Nun who received the office of being the *tourière*, would, generally, be in charge of two things: 1. If the bell on the outside was rung, she would go to *the turn* on inside of the enclosure, and, in some cases, speak to the guest standing on the other side while being hidden behind the turn. 2. She would retrieve the donations (e.g. food) that were placed in the turn for the community by the faithful. "The turn" was a small to large wooden round "box" on a turn-style, which was hollow with shelves inside to allow those on the outside to place donations or letters, etc, on it. When the turn was *turned,* these donations would then be on the inside of the cloistered side of the monastery. In Carmel, at least, there could also be a turn in the sacristy, so that the Sister Sacristan could put all the items she had prepared for Mass inside of it, and deliver these to the priest without being seen, or communicated with.

4 Abbé Blond, Vicar General of Beauvais, published a well-documented biography of Madame Thouret, Sister [Charlotte] of the Resurrection, accompanied by a portrait: the only one we have from the group of Carmelite martyrs; in-**8°**, 1898, Desclée, de Brouwer et Cie.

entered in 1734, took the habit in 1736, and made her profession in 1737. For many years, she served as Sacristan. Even in her old age, she retained the humility and spirit of obedience and submission of a simple Novice.

The five Nuns who follow, without having been invested with dignities, will nonetheless each present a distinctive and interesting character. Their order of age was also their order of Profession. These were the Sisters Brard, Hanisset, Trézel, Chrétien, and Pelras.

Catherine-Charlotte Brard, known in religion as Sister Euphrasie of the Immaculate Conception, was born in Bourth, in the diocese of Evreux, on September 7, 1736. She entered Carmel at the age of twenty and took her vows a year later, in 1757. Both serious and pleasant, Queen Marie Leczinska, who enjoyed her conversation, called her "her most lovable and religious philosopher." She was nonetheless very quick-witted, and her cheerfulness and enthusiasm made her the soul of Recreation[5]. Letters of spiritual direction addressed to her by her superiors, even before 1789, show that she was eager for corporal mortifications, which they tried to temper. Despite her recognized merits, the votes of her Sisters did not entrust her with any official offices. She was not the last to be surprised by this: in her private correspondence with her superiors, she accuses herself of pride, jealousy, and a tendency to criticize. Was not spontaneously revealing these imperfections a sign of her willingness to correct them? One day, one of the Sisters expressed her surprise to Abbé Rigaud, Superior and Visitor General, that Sister Euphrasie had never been appointed to the dignity of Prioress: "My daughter,"

5 [TN] In Carmel, there are usually two periods of Recreation: one after Dinner (i.e. Lunch, or the main meal), and the other in the evening after Supper (or, Collation, on fasting days). Recreation would usually last about thirty minutes to an hour, during which the Nuns were allowed to break their silence and speak freely with one another, while keeping themselves occupied with some sort of handwork (sewing, etc). On Sundays or feast days, not being permitted to do handwork, they might take a walk outside, etc.

replied Monsieur Rigaud, "there are souls whose salvation can only be achieved in a state of humility, abjection, and complete dependence, and this state, believe me, is the only one that suits this Sister." Let us not abuse these confidences to judge this Nun: she knew herself, she fought herself in secret: and even before her final sacrifice, she will have the joy of overcoming herself.

Wisdom, prudence, and discernment characterized Marie-Anne Hanisset, known in religion as Sister Thérèse of the Heart of Mary. Born in Reims in 1742, she took her vows in 1764. For many years, to the satisfaction of her Sisters, she served as the primary *tourière* and the sub-treasurer.

Marie-Gabrielle Trézel, known in religion as Sister Thérèse of Saint Ignatius, was originally from Compiègne: there she had her family, one member of which, as we shall see, sadly became involved in the revolutionary groups in the town. Born on April 4, 1743, she entered Carmel on July 15, 1770, and took her vows on December 12, 1771. Without the aid of any book, she would remain before the altar as if in conversation with God: the community called her "the Hidden Treasure." Sister Marie of the Incarnation recounts the following anecdote about her: «Our Mother Prioress having communicated to us her intention to gather three or four sisters with her for a competition of silence, I said to her: 'My dear Mother, we must include my Sister Saint Ignatius.' — 'Let us be careful,' said Mother, 'for she alone would win the palm.' And she added: "I say this with all the more conviction because, for my part, I can assure you that I have never seen her break the silence." We can see that at the Carmel of Compiègne, piety did not exclude good humor or innocent mischief.

The greater part of the Nuns entered the convent at the age of twenty, giving God the first fervor of their hearts. This was not the case for Rose Chrétien de la Neuville. Born in Evreux on December 30, 1741, she felt, from her First Communion, a deep attraction to religious life. Nevertheless, she resisted, and, as if to radically triumph over a thought that was becoming an obsession, she accepted the hand of a first cousin for whom, moreover, she felt some inclination. After six years, this union was broken by the death of her husband, M. Chrétien de la Neuville. The grief of the young widow was profound, violent, and desperate: manifesting itself in ways that bordered on the strange. She shut herself in her room, never leaving, receiving no visitors, not even from her family, and interacting with her servants only to give them orders. Even her room was draped in black curtains. She had abandoned her devotional practices and devoted herself to the reading of novels and plays. To shake her out of this deplorable hypochondria, one of her uncles, M. de la Vaulx, the chief cantor of Avranches[6] Cathedral (she lived near that town), tried to see her but the door remained closed. He wrote to her and received no reply.

Two years passed in this way. Her uncle did not lose heart and renewed his attempts and prayers for his niece. She finally gave orders to let him in if he returned. Informed of her disposition, he hastened to come. When she saw him, she burst into tears: he was no less moved than she was. Little by little, with persuasive skill and great tact, he persuaded his niece to remove the black curtains she had surrounded herself with, to receive her close relatives, to give up the frivolous reading that was causing her to lose sight of her duties, and even to return to her studies of music and drawing. Thus, finally, the principles of religion in which she had been raised would once again become the nourishment and direction of her life.

One last avowal remained for her to make, one intimate resolution to reveal. Remaining faithful, despite everything, to her first desires of her childhood, she told her uncle that she wanted to enter religious life, and, to hasten the fulfillment of her plan, she asked him to go to Saint-Denis and seek the advice of Mother Thérèse of Saint Augustine. The august Carmelite granted her desire; she met with the uncle and,

6 *Sic* in the manuscript: M. Villecourt says: Evreux (p. 101).

some time later, received the postulant and offered to receive her within the convent of Saint-Denis. "But," said Sister Marie of the Incarnation, "having then discovered that the widow's means allowed her to provide a fairly substantial dowry, she designated our house (that of Compiègne), which she knew and was very fond of." Indeed, the Carmel of Compiègne was poor, while, as we shall see later, thanks to the presence of Princess Louise, the convent of Saint-Denis had recovered from its previous difficulties.

Rose Chrétien arrived at the Carmel of Compiègne on June 14, 1776[7] and took the habit on September 12th of that year. Her period of novitiate must have been fraught with interior struggles against herself, judging by what her exterior attitude seemed to betray. "The cold and disdainful mood of this dear Sister," said Sister Marie of the Incarnation, "contrasted infinitely with the frank and natural cheerfulness of her fellow young Novices, who constantly complained to their Mother Superior about the discomfort and constraint that, they said, the *sullen* air of this older Sister caused them, adding: 'Ah, dear Mother, how we wish that God would allow her to become disgusted or not be received at the Chapter! We do not know if Heaven will grant our wish, but we pray for it nonetheless.' And the Mother would say to them as often as the complaints were repeated: 'Patience, patience, my children, let the good God do as He wills, He knows more than we do, and be content to desire and ask for your companion the fulfillment of His Holy Will.'" Let us add that during her novitiate, as indeed later on, she confided to none of her companions that she had been married; even her Novice Mistress was unaware of this: only the Mother Prioress knew, and she too kept silent.

7 At least, that is the date generally accepted. Born in 1741, she would have been thirty-five years old at the time. So, assuming that she had married at the age of 18 or 20 and been widowed after six years, that is, at the age of 24 or 26, with the two more years spent in the sickly state of mind we have described, she would have let five or seven whole years pass before entering Carmel. The date of 1770 seems more likely to us, but as yet, there is insufficient evidence.

At last, probably in 1777 (as the date has not been preserved), she pronounced her vows. As if this solemn moment marked the end of such violent inner turmoil, which she had been unable to hide from her companions, she underwent a complete transformation. She was no longer the same person. "Having become humble, gentle, and affable, she was seen to be striding along the path to perfection; equally ingenious in mortifying her senses as she had been in satisfying them, but at the same time full of kindness, attention, and deference toward her Sisters, always ready to oblige them and even going so far as to compose verses, short plays, and decorations for the feasts of her Mother Superiors and the Sisters celebrating their jubilees."

Should we summarize the visible unfolding of the designs of God for this soul? After an initial call which she resisted, He satisfied her desires only to confound her; He abandons her to herself, He brings her low; then, through rebellions triumphed by a will aided by grace, He brought her back into His arms, humiliated, defeated, but happy and finally showing it in the outward and joyful harmony of her faculties.

Such was the story of Rose Chrétien de la Neuville, known in religion as Sister Julie.

Mother Marie-Henriette of Providence, born Anne Pelras, was born in Cajarc (Lot) on June 17, 1760; she was therefore one of the youngest Sisters in the community. Of the twelve children her parents had, one of the boys became a priest, and the three eldest daughters entered the Congregation of the Daughters of Charity of Nevers. Anne Pelras was one of them. She was only fifteen or sixteen at the time; "but," says Sister Marie of the Incarnation, "as nature had endowed her with all the charms a woman could possess, her uncommon beauty exposed her to dangers that alarmed her modesty. She therefore believed she had to renounce the world altogether in order to keep herself safe. And, with her already very strong inclination for the cloister, she presented herself to our Mothers at the age of twenty-five on March 26, 1785, took the

Holy Habit that coming October, and pronounced her vows on October 22, 1786. Our Sister's knowledge and, even more so, her extreme prudence led to her being appointed assistant infirmarian almost immediately, a position she filled until the last moment with truly admirable zeal and charity."

Six other Choir Nuns, who were part of the community in 1789, were later separated from it either by natural death or by other circumstances. Sister Marie of the Incarnation barely mentions them, and the documents of the Carmel are almost completely missing. We will not omit them. They had shared the life, the vows, and the hopes of their Sisters; like them, they had promised themselves to the sacrifice[8] and were only spared from it by the will of Providence.

The eldest and longest Professed Nun of this group, Madame Boitel, known in religion as Sister Elisabeth of Jesus-Mary, was born in Clermont (Oise) in 1716. She had a nephew who was a Carmelite, a niece at the *Hôtel-Dieu* of Abbeville, and a sister at the Carmel of Amiens. Another of her sisters had entered the Carmel of Compiègne. Madame Boitel entered with her, less out of a personal vocation than to help her sister settle in. But her sister did not settle in, while Madame Boitel remained. She took her vows in 1737. At the time of our story, she was seventy-three years old and suffering from serious infirmities.

Marie-Louise Legros, Sister Henriette-Emmanuel-Stanislas of Providence, originally from Rosières-en-Santerre, was born on October 18, 1735, and took her vows on August 15, 1757.

We do not know the surname of Sister Anne-Marie-Xavier of the Resurrection. Born in 1739, she appears to have taken her vows in 1763.

Marie-Josèphe d'Hangest, Sister Pierre of Jesus, also born in Rosières in 1742, was undoubtedly related to Louis-Gabriel

8 [TN] Referring to the act of consecration all the Sisters had made in the last months of 1792, to offer themselves up to Our Lord as victim souls to make atonement for France as martyrs. See Chapter 5.

d'Hangest, a former musketeer, who would later appear (13 and 14 Floréal Year II – May 2 and 3, 1794) before the Revolutionary Tribunal of Paris for defending the Tuileries on August 10th and who would be sentenced to death.[9] We do not know the date of her entry into Carmel nor of her profession.

The same is true of Marie-Elisabeth Jourdain, Sister Thérèse of Jesus, of whom we know but the date of her birth: December 17, 1749.

We already know, from her own writings, about Sister Marie of the Incarnation, born Françoise-Geneviève Philippe, in Paris on November 16, 1761, and baptized the following day at the Church of Saint-Nicolas-des-Champs.[10]

Monsieur Villecourt (*Preface,* p. 24) says of this Sister, regarding the persecutions she would later suffer: "It is useless to explain the causes of this fury that was directed particularly against her. One can not ignore that there were certain classes that were more cruelly persecuted at that time, and, unfortunately for Sister Marie of the Incarnation, her birth was known,[11] which, in the eyes of the law, was an even greater crime than her state as a Nun." Elsewhere, in the same *Preface* (p. 21), we continue to read: "The brilliant education that she had received, her family's connections with the greatest and most illustrious figures in the world, seemed to prepare her to play a role that was all the more flattering in that she could grace the most beautiful societies with the natural and acquired talents with which her mind

9 In the 16th century, there was a d'Hangest who was Bishop of Noyon.

10 "Daughter of Pierre-Martin PHILIPPE and Marie-Madeleine JOLIVET, his wife, bourgeois of Paris, residing on Rue des Fontaines. The godfather, François Pigeot, a baker, residing in Faubourg of Saint-Antoine; the godmother, Geneviève Bresseno, residing on *Rue des Fontaines,* who signed with us." Extract from the Baptismal record, in the Archives of the Oise department.

11 [EN] The writer suggests that Sister Marie of the Incarnation might have been an illegitimate daughter of Louis XV, and that such a fact was publicly known.

was adorned." What can we conclude from these lines, which are as enigmatic as they are transparent? According to her baptismal certificate, Françoise-Geneviève was born in Paris, on *Rue des Fontaines,* in the parish of Saint-Nicolas-des-Champs, where she was baptized, with a baker as her godfather; her father, whose profession is not indicated, was absent. Another document states that she was from L'Isle-Adam and originated from Pontoise, where her entire family lived. If she was actually born in L'Isle-Adam, could she have been taken to Paris for her baptism? Should we infer from this vague information that she had mysterious and royal origins?

Around 1782, at the age of twenty or twenty-one, in Vernon, where she was boarding at a convent, she was struck by a nervous disorder that manifested itself in convulsions and paralysis. She was taken, or rather carried, to Pontoise to her family. Her infirmity was well known; not only did her limbs refuse to function, but her stomach could not retain any food, even liquids. The skill of the surgeons and three doctors were powerless. At that time, the apostolic process for the beatification of Madame Acarie was underway in Pontoise. The sufferer, who was in communication with the Carmel in Pontoise through a cousin, Sister Saint John of the Cross, who was the Prioress there, decided to undertake a novena in honor of the Venerable,[12] and to have herself carried to her tomb on July 16, 1784, the Feast of Our Lady of Mount Carmel, and to receive Communion there. She promised that, if she were healed, she would enter Carmel. The Reverend Mother Prioress and her sisters joined in the intention of this novena.

When the day arrived, Mademoiselle Philippe arrived in a chair at five o'clock in the morning. She was placed in front of the chapel of the Venerable, from where she heard Mass. After the community had received Holy Communion, the officiant approached her chair; but the patient was in such a state of collapse that he did not dare to give her the Holy Host, fearing that she would expire before receiving

12 [TN] Madame Acarie

It. She was trembling all over and sweat in abundance was pouring down her cheeks. However, she had the strength to reassure the priest, and as he was about to place the Host on her tongue, she pronounced the words of the paralytic in the Gospel: "Jesus, Son of David, have mercy on me." During the rest of the Mass, she remained still as if she had fainted.

But, no sooner had the priest descended the steps of the altar when young Philippe jumped up from her chair, exclaiming, "*I am healed!*" She advanced into the sanctuary, prostrated herself before the tomb of Madame Acarie, then, climbing eight steps, she knocked on the grille[13] of the Nuns, repeating to them, "I am healed," and inviting them to give thanks to God with her. She spent the day at the monastery, kneeling during all the Masses, eating the food that was offered to her, and showing herself to the crowd, which continued to arrive until nine o'clock in the evening to see the miracle. Despite the prognosis of the doctor, who believed it was merely what he called a "spiritual spasm," two years passed for Mademoiselle Philippe without any relapse in her health. She then fulfilled her promise to enter Carmel. Assigned to the monastery of Compiègne, she entered on September 23, 1786, took the Habit on March 23, 1787, and made her Profession on July 22, 1788, under the name of Marie of the Incarnation, in gratitude to the Venerable Madame Acarie, who bore that name and whose intercession had obtained her cure.

We will often mention the name of this Sister; for, although she did not share in the martyrdom of her companions, Providence seemed to have kept her apart so that she could become their historiographer: what would we know about most of them if Sister Marie of the Incarnation had not

13 [TN] In the chapel of a Carmelite monastery there is a large metal grille, a sort of "fence" that makes it difficult to see the Nuns, and which separates the chapel of the Nuns from that of the public and of the sanctuary. Customarily, there is additionally an opaque black curtain drawn across this grille on the inside, as well as wooden-shutters, which serve to completely hide the Nuns from sight. Hence, why Mademoiselle Phillipe would have had to knock on the grille to get their attention.

collected and written down her memories?

Let us return to the Nuns who completed the sacred battalion.

There were three Converse Sisters, or Nuns of the white veil: Antoinette Roussel, Sister [Marie] of the Holy Ghost, born in Fresne, near Claye, in the Diocese of Meaux, on August 4, 1742, entered Carmel at the age of twenty-five, professed at twenty-seven (May 14, 1769), with a very lively and active character, but whose habitual suffering hindered her good will; Marie Dufour, Sister Saint Martha, born in Beaune on October 1, 1742; she entered at the age of thirty and continued in perfecting herself upon the examples of piety which she had received in her family; Juliette Vérolot, Sister Saint-François [Xavier], born in Laignes, in the Diocese of Autun, on January 11, 1764, the youngest of the Sisters and the last of the Community to be admitted to pronounce her vows. It was January 12, 1789: she had turned twenty-five the day before. "Our Mother," said Sister Marie of the Incarnation, "felt she should, before our Sister made her commitment, place before her eyes the reality of the misfortunes that were threatening the religious orders. — 'Ah, my dear good Mother,' she said with her ordinary naivety, 'you can rest assured; for, as long as I have the happiness of being consecrated to my God, that is all I desire. So, my dear good Mother (that was her expression), do not worry about me at all, because, really, God will take care of me.'"

The youngest member of the monastery was Marie-Geneviève Meunier, born in Saint-Denis, near Paris, on May 28, 1766. She entered Carmel on May 29, 1788, and took the habit on December 30th of that year, taking the name Sister Constance. She was to remain a Novice: despite the effort of her parents, and despite the events that were unfolding, she proved herself worthy of her name[14] and remained so until the end. She was twenty-three years old in 1789.

14 [EN] "*Constance*" means steadfastness in French.

It is with the two Externs that this nomenclature will come to an end. They were neither Nuns, nor Converse Sisters, nor Novices, but simply domestic servants; it was their piety rather than self-interest that had attached them to the house. Catherine and Thérèse Soiron, originally from Compiègne (their father was a turner there), were respectively forty-seven and thirty-eight years old in 1789. Catherine had been appointed the first Extern at the age of thirty in 1772. The other, although younger, must have been named as the second Extern during the same period, for it was she who, in 1772, had been sent to meet Mademoiselle Lidoine when she had left Paris to go to the monastery of Compiègne[15]. During one of her visits, the Princess de Lamballe[16] had the opportunity to see Thérèse Soiron: struck by her beauty and grace, she wanted to attach her to her person: "Be sure," she said to her, "that I will love you well and make your life as happy as possible." But Thérèse Soiron did not let herself be coaxed, and declared that she preferred the place where God had put her. Her fidelity and that of her sister was unwavering. In a letter from 1788, the Mother Prioress already referred to her as "our dear sister Thérèse." She was a sister, in effect, without vows, without a habit, without any obligation of conscience. If, at that time, they were both given this name, could it be refused when they were seen to be faithful until death to the community that had adopted them?

---

15 Letter from the Mother Prioress to Mademoiselle de Grand-Rut, November 10, 1788. Villecourt, p. 124.

16 [EN] One of the wealthiest and most famous noblewomen of the time.

CHAPTER III

THE DECLARATION OF AUGUST 5, 1790

The *cahiers* (reports) submitted to the Estates General foreshadowed measures against congregations and convents: the Constituent Assembly did not disappoint this expectation. One reads in the preamble to the Constitution, "The law no longer recognizes religious vows or any other commitment that is contrary to natural rights or the Constitution." In this declaration, the terms of which were even renewed in the recent law of July 1, 1901, we immediately see the idea of removing the civil effect of religious vows in order to restrict them to the realm of one's own personal conscience. Those with foresight, and especially those concerned, had reason to be somewhat worried. How did this strange principle so quickly lead to the suppression of congregations? Budgetary difficulties, hostility towards everything related to the Church or religion, and the desire to revolutionize the state and to undermine and destroy what had hitherto formed the foundation of French society, were to strike at the very roots of the monastic tree and bring it down abruptly.

On October 26, 1789, they began by suspending the taking of vows, and, to show their haste, the Assembly decided that the law would be submitted immediately to the King for his approval and sent to all the tribunals and monasteries. Moreover, it made no secret of the fact that the suppression of religious congregations was approaching, but that, for the moment, the question was reserved. The monastery of Compiègne immediately felt the effects of this law. Sister Constance, née Meunier, had taken the habit on December 13, 1788, and was expecting to pronounce her vows in December of 1789. "Pray much for your little companion, Constance," wrote the Mother Prioress on the 15th, "Alas! I should have had the consolation of receiving her vows today, were it not for the decree that was legally served on me three weeks ago. This poor child is very sad; her mother wants to take her back. We are opposed to this, but I fear that she will prevail. It will be a terrible ordeal for this child. *Fiat! Fiat!*"[1] Her brother came, in fact, supplied with an authorization from her parents, to take her away by force, but the young Novice resisted. The commissioner and the royal prosecutor intervened without success, and had to acknowledge that, being in full possession of her faculties, Sister Constance did not intend to renounce a freely made resolution and that she accepted all the consequences. She was 23 years old; the first and the youngest, and without being religiously committed, to set an example of unwavering perseverance.

The legislature then relentlessly attacked ecclesiastical property and religious men and women, seeking to hasten the fall and dissolution of the ecclesiastical structure. On November 2, all such property was placed at the disposal of the Nation, that is to say, it was generally confiscated. On the 13th, owners, referred to as *holders,*[2] as if their possession were precarious, were required to declare their immoveable and moveable assets.[3] On January 16, 1790, the deadline for this declaration was extended. On February 5, one out of every two religious houses of the same Order, two out of every three, and three out of every four, when located in the same city, were suppressed, "pending", as the law frankly states, "more considerable suppressions." They moved forward quickly; on February 13, monastic vows were prohibited for both sexes, with a ban on ever reestablishing them in the future. Thanks to an amendment by Abbé de Montesquiou, who, incidentally, had voted in favor of the principle of the law, Nuns were allowed to remain in the houses where they were currently living; they were even expressly exempted from the article which obliged religious to consolidate several houses into one.

1 [EN] *Fiat voluntas tua,* "Thy will be done."

2 [TN] *"détenteurs"*

3 [TN] Real estate and personal property.

It was a time when theater, literature, and public forums resounded with lamentations about the "cloistered victims;" when philosophers pretended to free them from tyrannies of all kinds and, by opening the convents considered as prisons, restore them to freedom. However, Abbé de Montesquiou said before the Assembly: "So far, I have received only letters and requests from Nuns who want to remain in their cloisters." The Prioresses of the Carmels of Paris and Saint-Denis submitted a petition to the National Assembly: "Deign to inform yourselves, Gentlemen, of the life led in all the communities of our Order: do not believe either the opinions of the multitude nor the fears of humanity. People like to publish worldwide that monasteries are nothing more than prisons for victims slowly consumed by remorse, but we protest before God that, if there is true happiness on earth, we enjoy it in the shadow of the sanctuary, and that if we had to choose again between the secular world and the cloister, none of us would hesitate to confirm our first choice with even greater joy…It is in the name of all our Sisters, whose monasteries are scattered throughout the different regions of the kingdom, that we, Gentlemen, have the honor of placing this request at your feet. Each one has signed, and would have liked to do so with her own blood, preferring a thousand deaths to a change in her state in life, which would be her martyrdom. The testimonies of their fidelity are in the hands of a deputy of your august Assembly, who will produce them when you order him to do so.[4]" This deputy was Bp. de Bonal, the Bishop of Clermont.

Vain reasonings, vain pleas! The Assembly ignored them.

What concerns for a Prioress arose from these uncertainties! In ordinary times, the burden is heavy, but the trust and zeal of her companions lighten the load. Watching over herself, watching over others; maintaining regularity, preventing

4 D'Hesmivy d'Auribeau: *Mémoires pour servir à l'histoire de la persécution française* (Memoirs to serve as a history of the French persecution).. Rome, 1795, Part II, pp. 655, 657.

relaxation, nurturing piety, restraining the most ardent in their thirst for mortifications; attending to and observing the health of all; not neglecting the material interests of the house, however modest they may be; keeping in correspondence with the superiors or with other monasteries: such are the cares that suffice to overwhelm a soul! Yet she must draw additional strength from the meditations customary at Carmel in order to recollect herself, know herself, and in the midst of so many tasks, not lose sight of furthering her own perfection. The tact of the Prioress of Compiègne, her prudence, her already long experience of being Prioress, the decisiveness of her character, the fervor of her piety, all these gifts were further enriched by an uncommon education that would greatly facilitate many of her duties.

To these daily responsibilities, circumstances added new obligations that were no less serious. What would become of this monastery, where she had lived for fifteen years, which had existed for a century and a half, renowned for the piety of its Nuns, for its royal and princely connections, and for its eminent regularity? Would it be swept up in the general ruin of religious orders that so many decrees were so openly announcing? Stripped of their possessions, what would become of her Nuns? Alongside and far above these earthly concerns, was there not reason to fear for the Nuns' return into the world? Should they be consigned to exile, as had been done in 1783 with those in Belgium, whom French laws were now forcing to return to their country of origin, where the laws had improved? Should they be delivered up to the perils of life in France, in the midst of revolution, scattered, and deprived of the strength of community life? What problems! What anxiety! What responsibilities!

Nevertheless, the exercises[5] continued as usual and

---

5 [TN] The *community exercises*: all of the ceremonies, prayers, customs, and communal functions that order and define the daily life of a Carmelite. (e.g. the ceremonies before and after meals, the Divine Office, the times of mental prayer, the times of recreation, Chapter, etc.)

community feasts were celebrated as normal. Such was the case for the fiftieth anniversary of Profession for Mother Charlotte of the Resurrection: Anne Thouret, that infirmarian, Sub-Prioress, and treasurer, whose health had been worn down by her service to the community. The law suppressing the religious Orders had struck her more painfully than anyone else. Almost eighty years old and half-crippled, could one have fathomed any future for her other than a peaceful, quiet, and undramatic existence?

According to custom, with veil raised[6], she had attended Mass with a sermon reserved for her. Many of the friends of Compiègne had congratulated her in the parlor[7]. In the monastery, all her companions had rejoiced to see this matriarch, this doyenne of the community, whose years had increased her merits and good examples. "She could perceive," said Sister Marie of the Incarnation, "from the enthusiasm and delight that burst forth, how much she was loved, cherished, and respected."

This joy was soon followed by mourning. It was around this time (April 1790) that Mother Anne-Marie-Xavier of the Resurrection died: she was only fifty-one years old, and twenty-seven years professed. We know her only through the two or three lines we are borrowing from a letter of the Mother Prioress dated August 14, 1790: "It is not my Sister Elisabeth, but my Sister Xavier whom we lost last April: her death has left a great void...I hope she is praying for us in

6 [TN] Either that the curtain was unveiled from the chapel's grille, or that she assisted at Mass without her veil lowered to cover her face.

7 [TN] The speak-room. This was a room where meetings with those on the outside of the enclosure took place: for example, when the Sisters met with their family members, or conferences were given by a priest, etc. Just as in the chapel, the parlor was divided between the enclosure and the outside by a metal grille, opaque black curtain, and wooden shutters with lock and key. Customarily, after the shutters were opened, the opaque black curtain would only be drawn back for family members, or very special occasions, possibly like this one. Other than that, guests spoke with the Nuns without being able to see them..

Heaven."[8]

However, on March 20, 1790, the Constituent Assembly had just ruled that the municipalities would take an inventory of the assets of the monasteries and that each Monk or Nun would be interrogated regarding their intention to remain in their convent or to leave it. To remain there was an illusion! Already, many houses had been suppressed and their doors shut: so much for the monks. As for the Nuns, despite the promises of the law of February 13, how could the same fate not have threatened them? Inventorying their property was the signal for its confiscation. Its management even passed to the municipalities, and Nuns as well as Monks were left with only a pension payable by the State. Furthermore, the municipalities had to go to the monasteries, gather together either the Nuns or the Monks, inform them of the supposed benefits that the Revolution would bring them, and question them about their intentions. To assure the independence and freedom of their answers, each Monk and each Nun had to be interrogated separately, without their superiors or companions present. A secretary would record their statements. It was surely hoped that, faced with this solemn ordeal, a number of Nuns would renounce their vows and eagerly return to a freedom that they were reputed to have relinquished only under duress.

On August 4, 1790, the members of the *Directoire* (District Board) of Compiègne — Messrs. de Pronnay, the president and a former member of the Order of Cluny, from a Compiègne family that had given a Nun to Carmel; Poulain, the public prosecutor; Bertrand, the secretary, a bookseller and printer; and Joly and Scellier Jr., the latter of whom we will discuss later — all arrived at the monastery and proceeded to inventory the effects, silverware, coins, books, and papers, leaving the rest in the care and custody of the Nuns.

---

8 Letter to Mademoiselle de Grand-Rut (*Histoire des Religieuses de Compiègne* (History of the Nuns of Compiègne), etc., p. 144).

They returned the next day and, after exploring the entire house, chose the large community room as the most suitable location. Four soldiers were posted as sentries at the two doors of the room; the others were posted at the doors of the cells and cloisters. The Nuns were called in one by one and interrogated separately. To each one, the President announced that he was bringing deliverance and invited her to speak without fear and to declare whether she wanted to leave the house and return to her family. All replied in the same way: but, in order to take note of the steadfastness shown by each of them, it is necessary to reproduce these statements *verbatim*, as the secretary collected them from their mouths and transcribed them in the minutes.

Madame Lidoine, the Prioress, appeared first. She declared that she "desired to live and die in this holy house."

Madame Brideau, the Sub-Prioress: "Her desire is to live and die as a Carmelite."

Next came the two doyennes: Madame Piedcourt and Madame Thouret. Madame Piedcourt declared that, "as a Carmelite for 56 years, she would like nothing more in the world than to have yet the same number of years to devote to the Lord;" Madame Thouret, "that she wants to live and die in her state."

The statement by Madame Brard, this Nun who had such a quick wit that one might have suspected her of some tendencies to insubordination, testified on the contrary to the determination and zeal of her soul: "A Nun of her own free will and choice, she is firmly resolved to keep her habit, even if she has to pay for this happiness with her blood."

Madame Legros: "that she finds no greater happiness than to live as a Carmelite, and that her most ardent desire is to live and die as such."

Madame d'Hangest: "that if she had a thousand lives, she would consecrate them to the state in life she has embraced, and that nothing could persuade her to leave the house where she lives and where she has found happiness."

Madame de Croissy, Sister Henriette of Jesus, a former Prioress, now Mistress of Novices, declared: "that she has made her vows for life, and that she eagerly seizes this occasion to renew these pledges." A few moments before appearing, she had written three stanzas in which she vividly expressed her contempt for worldly life and her love and joy in the cloistered life. She placed them before the eyes of her questioners, who left this intrepid profession on the table.

Madame Hanisset declared: "that if she could double the bonds that bind her to God, she would do so with all the strength and joy that depend on her."

Madame Trézel, the "Hidden Treasure," simply said that she was content with her state and that she wanted to live and die in it.

Madame Jourdain declared that her intention was to die a Carmelite.

Madame Chrétien, that widow who was so proud at first and later so amiable to her Sisters, declared that she wanted to remain in this holy house for the rest of her life.

Madame Pelras: "that she wants to remain in this house; that such is the wish of her heart."

Madame Philippe, Sister Marie of the Incarnation: "that she wants to live and die in her state in life; that her happiness is as constant as the motives of her vocation."

Madame Boitel, whose infirmities prevented her from signing, declared: "that she wants to live and die a true Carmelite; that after the Heavenly Homeland, there is no deeper happiness."

Such were the declarations of the fifteen Choir Nuns: unanimous declarations, some very simple, as if emanating from a conviction that needed no embellishment to express itself; others more animated, testimony to a more ardent temperament that wanted to manifest both the firmness of their decision and their revolt against a useless and impertinent question. All these statements are signed in the official minutes with their family name and religious name.

The statements of the three Converse Sisters are in keeping with those of the Choir Nuns: Sister Roussel declared that she wanted to live and die in her holy state and in this holy house; Sister Dufour, that she wanted to live and die in her holy state; Sister Vérolot, the last to have made Profession (January 12, 1789), "that a well-born wife remains with her spouse, and that nothing can make her abandon her Divine Spouse, Our Lord Jesus Christ."

Constance Meunier, not having been admitted to Profession and remaining a Novice, had no declaration to make; as for the two Externs, Catherine and Thérèse Soiron, they were not Nuns: the district considered them only as servants.

However much confidence the Mother Prioress may have had in advance in the firmness of her companions, she must have felt great joy at their unanimity. This joy was shared by her Sisters. What strength for the present, what assurance for the future, was this confirmation of the generous sentiments shared by all! What solidarity of resolve! In their petition to the Constituent Assembly, the Carmelites of Paris and of Saint-Denis had declared that "if their Sisters were called upon to choose between the world and the cloister, there would be none who would not ratify their first choice with even greater joy." The ordeal proved them right: if the Carmelites of Compiègne endured it with honor, it is fair to recall that the same was true in all the Carmels of France: Abbé d'Hesmivy d'Auribeau asserts that, out of the 1,900 Nuns of this Order, only five or six defected. The legislators' predictions were proved wrong: the strictest Order was also the most faithful and best equipped for the fight.

CHAPTER IV

THE EXPULSION (SEPTEMBER 14, 1792)

The declaration required of the Nuns was only a first step: the civil authorities claimed to have control even over the government of their communities. "We wanted," they said in Compiègne, "to have a Prioress of our own choosing." Soon, a law of October 8-14, 1790, ordered municipalities to proceed, in the presence of a municipal officer, with the election of a superior and a treasurer. A decree of that December 8-12 decided, contrary to the custom of the monasteries, that the Converse Sisters would participate in the vote.

Consequently, on January 11, 1791, two municipal officers, Le Cornier and Mouton, went to the Carmelite monastery, entered inside, and assembled all the Nuns, the Converse Sisters included. Madame Boitel, confined to her cell[1] by her infirmities, did not attend the meeting. They proceeded with the election: 16 out of 17 votes elected Madame Lidoine as superior (we know that she already was): Madame de Croissy, Mother Henriette of Jesus, a former Prioress and currently Mistress of Novices, was elected treasurer. The Converse Sisters Dufour and Roussel signed the minutes; Sister Vérollot did not sign, perhaps because she did not know how. Thus, this election in the presence of municipal officials was nothing more than an act of intrusive interference whence notably manifested the perfect unity between the Choir and Converse Nuns, and the unanimity of their feelings for their superiors. A few weeks later (February 20, 1791), Madame Boitel died, expressing regret not for dying, but for being snatched away by death from the trials and martyrdom she foresaw, or rather expected, for her Sisters and herself.

This was the time when the intrusion of the Constitutional Bishops and Priests was causing turmoil in the parishes and

1 [TN] What the bedroom of a Carmelite Nun is called.

inaugurating those religious struggles that the Constituent Assembly had so recklessly added to the social and political struggles. If the Mother Prioress received any news from the Carmels in France, she may have learned that in Verdun, the Prioress had turned away Aubry, the intruder bishop[2] of the Meuse, and that he had not dared to force open their cloister; that in Besançon, the intruder bishop, Séguin, had been received neither by the Carmelites, nor by the Benedictines, nor by the Nuns of other Orders; that in Arles, the intruder bishop, Roux, had suffered a similar affront at the Carmel. In Nantes, on the night of June 3-4, 1791, upon the refusal made by the Carmelites of Les Couëts[3] to receive Bishop Minée, the women of that area, joined by "patriotic" ladies of the bourgeoisie, committed acts of outrageous violence against the Nuns, which, for a long time caused them to be put to shame and referred to as the *fouetteuses* des Couëts.[4]

It does not appear that in Compiègne, the intruder bishop of Oise, Massieu, former curé[5] of Cergy, made any attempt of this kind. Were there even gatherings and popular riots around the monastery? Did they experience, as in so many other places, those abusive, insulting visits from the municipalities, the National Guard, shameless shrews, or a blind mob? No document mentions such things; there is even silence from Sister Marie of the Incarnation, who, during that

2 [EN] "*évêque intrus,*" the term by which the schismatic bishops, illegitimately appointed by the French government, were designated by faithful Catholics.

3 [TN] Since 1477, there existed in a place known as "Les Couëts", near to Nantes, a monastery of *Calced* Carmelites established by Blessed Françoise d'Amboise, Duchess of Brittany, with the support of Blessed John Soreth, the General of the Order at that time. This Carmel continued until the Revolution. This is likely the Carmelites that are referred to here. Whereas the first *Discalced* Carmelite Monastery was established in 1618 at the request of a family from Nantes.

4 [TN] *The whippers of Les Couëts* — Alfred Lallié: *Minée et son épiscopat.* (Minée and his bishopric). Review of the Revolution, v. 11, p. 31.

5 [TN] Pastor.

year of 1791, was in Compiègne, at the monastery, sharing the life of her Sisters, and therefore is an authoritative witness. To whom should we attribute this moderation? To [Bishop] Massieu, who was disinterested in his Diocese? To the curés of Compiègne who, although jurors,[6] were more weak than malicious? To the municipality, which was not concerned with aggravating laws that they were required to enforce?

In Compiègne, in the parish of Saint-Jacques, there was an association of ladies who, under the name of the *Charité de Saint-Jacques* (The Charity of Saint James), distributed aid to the poor, visited and nursed the sick, taught children, and fed the destitute. This institution dated back to the end of the seventeenth century. It had been inaugurated under the care of Claude Boucher of Essonville, the pastor of the parish, under the presidency of Bp. Brullard de Sillery, the Bishop of Soissons, in the presence of Mesdames de Maintenon, d'Harcourt, and de Beauvilliers, as well as a large number of charitable ladies from the town, regardless of their parish. There was a superior, assistants, a treasurer, and six Sisters of Charity, three of whom lived on site and three elsewhere. The Carmelites were no strangers to this work of charity: they contributed either through alms or by making clothes for the poor. The ladies of the town willingly came to foster their love for the poor among the humble and fervent daughters of Saint Teresa. We would like to quote the names that we read in the letters from the Nuns: Madame Pannelier, Madame and Mademoiselle Le Comier, Madame Maréchal, Madame de Lancry, and others, who, in the deprivation of faithful priests, still found in the monastery a chaplain, almoners, visitors of the Order, and priests whom circumstances had detached from their ordinary ministry. Thus, in the first rank, Abbé Courouble, a former member of the Society of Jesus,[7] a

6 [TN] Who took the schismatic oath to the Civil Constitution of the Clergy.

7 [EN] The Jesuits were suppressed in 1773 by Pope Clement XIV, under pressure from hostile Enlightenment monarchies.

chaplain and confessor of Carmel; Abbé de la Marche, who, without any special title, devoted himself to the ministry of souls; Abbé Rigaud, one of the general visitors of Carmel, who, although living in Paris, came from time to time to Compiègne and exercised a much sought-after ministry there; Abbé Bida, chaplain to the Carmelites of Reims; his father was the doctor of the convent; with respect to him, he had a particular appreciation for the Prioress, whose good advice had guided him towards the priesthood; he came from time to time to Carmel, either to say Mass or to preach[8]. His uncle, Abbé Jacquemart, a former Jesuit and a highly regarded director of the Carmelites of Reims, was known to the Nuns of Compiègne, as evidenced by a letter from Mother Henriette of Jesus. Finally, we see references to the curés of Belloy and Estrées, neighboring parishes which their pastors had been forced to abandon because they had refused to take the oath.[9]

Amidst the uncertainties, pains, and anxieties, a ray of joy shone upon the Carmel and upon the groups of pious ladies who frequented it. Pope Pius VI had already declared Venerable Madame Acarie, that valiant woman who had founded the Carmel of the Reform of Saint Teresa in France and who had given to it three of her daughters. On April 5, 1791, the Congregation of Rites gave a favorable opinion on the beatification. On the 24th, the Pope pronounced it; the

---

8 Abbé Bida would soon accompany the fifteen Carmelites of Reims to Belgium, and later to Paderborn in Westphalia. Throughout the entire time of their exile, he never abandoned them. He watched over their spiritual well-being as well as their modest material needs. He finally brought them back to Reims, (*Chroniques du Carmel; les Religieuses françaises en exil* (Chronicles of Carmel; the French Nuns in exile), by VICTOR PIERRE. The Review of Historical Questions, January 1903.)

9 The curé of Estrées-Saint-Denis from 1762 to 1791 was Monsieur Nicolas Prince, a native of Hainvillers, a canton of Ressons (Oise). He died in Montdidier in 1815 (Letter from Canon Pihan, curé of Estrées-Saint-Denis). There is some uncertainty about the name and identity of the curé of Belloy: was it Jean-Baptiste Vertu, appointed in 1786, or a certain Sir Vaillant, who signed numerous record entries in 1793 and 1795? (Letter from Monsieur Abbé Chrétien, curé of Ressons). Belloy is no longer a parish.

corresponding Brief appeared on May 24. On the Sunday within the Octave of the Ascension, the most pompous ceremonies took place at St. Peter's in Rome, in the presence of the Princesses of France, Mesdames Adélaïde and Victoire. Through the efforts of Cardinal de Bernis, who was still the ambassador of France, all the churches and convents of Rome were illuminated. The Pope allowed the same ceremony to be celebrated in all the Carmel churches. Was it possible for the monastery of Compiègne to give this event, so precious to the Order, the solemnity it deserved? The times hardly allowed it, but, even if it remained a private affair, the joy was no less intense.

A year had passed since the inventory of August 4, 1790, and the declaration of the following day. In March 1791, the Mother Treasurer had given the municipality a report of the finances, resources, and expenses of the monastery. The resources were very modest: they amounted to 7,963 livres, of which 3,022 had to be deducted for the chaplaincy, liturgical items, repairs, gardening and the gardener, the Extern Sisters, and the doctor. This left 4,941 livres for clothing, food, maintenance, and other expenses for 17 Nuns, 2 Extern Sisters, and 2 servants; or, 235 livres per person for twenty-one people.[10]

By an order of August 6, 1791, and pursuant to the law of October 14, 1790, the Directory only recognized fourteen Nuns and three Novices; it allocated 478 livres, 19 sous, and 8 deniers to each of the former, and 289 livres, 9 sous, and 8 deniers to each of the latter. These pensions were to be paid quarterly and in advance, starting on January 1, 1791. The advantage over the previous situation was only apparent, for these sums had to provide for not seventeen but twenty-one people, and in addition to cover the costs of the chaplaincy,

10 [EN] Historical studies of this time period estimate the average yearly salary of an unqualified worker to be between 250 and 300 livres per year. The sisters were effectively living on what could be considered a "minimum wage" for the standards of the time.

worship, maintenance, etc. These pensions could have been increased if the Nuns had agreed to let their house be sold. How could they agree to this? The monastery was their way of life, their community, their shelter: having the ability to remain there, they made use of it until the day, perhaps closer than they thought, when the law and force would overcome their resolve and their rights.

The elections for the Legislative Assembly (September 1791) in the department of Oise featured only the names of moderate men without any clear political leanings; the municipal elections were similar in character. Mr. de Cayrol, a lawyer and deputy at the tribunal of the district, was only elected mayor in the third round of voting with 78 votes out of 146 voters. A studious antiquarian and somewhat of a collector, he had undoubtedly given no decisive pledges to any party, which would explain his mediocre majority. The three curés of Compiègne – Desboves, curé of Saint-Jacques; Beaugrand, curé of Saint-Germain; and Thibaux, curé of Saint-Antoine – all three jurors, were elected; the first as a notable and the other two as municipal officers. Following the elections, the mayor, notables, assessors, municipal officers, and public prosecutor went as a group to the Church of Saint-Antoine and attended Mass there.

The year 1791 was therefore fairly peaceful, as were the first months of 1792. In the month of May of that year, the Mother Prioress believed she could travel to Paris. Abbé Rigaud, Superior General of the Carmelites, had summoned her there to discuss with her in person (as the postal service was unreliable) the precautions to be taken, the attitude to adopt in the face of future contingencies, and the agreement to be established between the houses of Carmel. He also wanted to give her some relics of Madame Acarie[11]. Upon her return to Compiègne, she soon learned of the decree of May 27, which

11 "This morning I saw Monsieur Rigaud, who gave me the box containing the relics of our blessed Sister. I will give you this repository next week." Letter from the Mother Prioress, dated Paris, May 16, 1792.

already ordered the deportation of priests: the shameful scenes of June 20, which had as their pretext the king's constant refusal to sanction this odious decree. The cries of hatred uttered in the Assembly against everything religious, the violent deportations of priests, carried out systematically by the departments, without any law authorizing them: what signs of an imminent and fatal outcome! The religious habit had already been declared illegal and prohibited twice. Sheltered behind their walls, the Carmelites were in no hurry to obey; the municipality did not insist.

On August 4, 1792, a letter was communicated to the Legislative Assembly in which commissioners sent to Soissons denounced the accumulation of federates[12] gathered there: "However," they said, «the houses of the *émigrés* remain vacant. An abbey of Notre-Dame, which could make a magnificent hospital, is occupied by forty-nine Nuns who could be transported elsewhere and who make this house a den of the most awful aristocracy." To which Charlier, from the Marne, replied: "I request that we immediately decree the precept that religious houses be evacuated and sold, and that we refer the matter to the Committee to set an increase in the pension proportional to the renting."[13] That was all it took to provoke a decision to that effect, and, with the help of the revolution of August 10, on the 17th, the Legislative Assembly issued the following decree:

> "Art. I. – By this October 1st, all the houses currently occupied by Nuns or Monks shall be vacated by the said Nuns and Monks, and shall be put up for sale at the discretion of the administrative bodies."

It was a far cry from the law of February 13, 1790, which allowed Nuns to remain in their houses, but what an illusion

12 [TN] The troops who volunteered for the French National Guard in the summer of 1792 during the French Revolution. The *fédérés* of 1792 effected a transformation of the Guard from a constitutional monarchist force into a republican revolutionary force.

13 Mon. v. XIII, p. 327 Reprint.

it would have been to imagine that this abnormal favor could be prolonged! Eliminating the congregations and maintaining the monasteries! Prohibiting the associations and allowing them to continue in practice! The contradiction was too great. Despite this law, how many communities of women had already had to disperse! The Mother Prioress immediately found places to stay in the city where she could distribute her companions. The municipality reminded her that the religious habit had long been prohibited and that new legal provisions no longer permitted a delay. Moreover, as they were henceforth destined to live a life in the world, it was prudent that they no longer wear clothing which, by distinguishing them, could cause them some trouble. They therefore forsook their holy liveries and donned secular clothing. The municipality proceeded to inventory the objects, including liturgical items, priestly vestments, monstrances, ciboriums, and all the precious furnishings that the convent had received from the generosity of queens, princes, and princesses. Not even the Nuns' personal belongings were spared, leaving them with only the bare necessities. Everything was taken away.

On September 12, they were ordered to evacuate the house immediately. The Mother Prioress had counted on the date of October 1st, which had been set by the decree, and had made her arrangements accordingly. The municipality insisted and granted only two days' delay. "It was on September 14, the day of the Exaltation of the Holy Cross," said Sister Marie of the Incarnation, "that we were torn from our dear and holy solitude."

A new life was opening up before them, but it was a retired life, a religious life where they would find Carmel even in this world to which they were forced to return.

CHAPTER V

AROUND THE CHURCH OF SAINT-ANTOINE

The community then consisted of twenty persons: fourteen Choir Nuns, three Converse Sisters known as Sisters of the white veil, Sister Constance, who remained a Novice, and the two Extern Sisters. "The fatal decree having been executed," said Sister Marie of the Incarnation, "it was agreed that, since we could not have the consolation of living together under the same roof, the community would be divided into four groups, and that the Externs would remain with us, so that they could deliver messages, buy provisions, and carry the food that was being prepared at the residence of the Mother Prioress to the three houses." The four "groups" were divided up as follows.

Through the mediation and care of Mr. Crouy, a surgeon, the Mother Superior rented from Madame Veuve[1] Saiget, residing at 9 Rue de Dampierre, now Rue Saint-Antoine, for 150 livres per year; this lady herself occupied part of the house as a tenant. This sublet included two rooms facing each other on the ground floor, two rooms on the first floor, and two others on the second floor, with views of the street and courtyard. This space was quite large, since, with the ground floor and the two upper floors, it comprised six rooms. The Mother Prioress reserved this domicile for herself and her group, which she composed as follows: Madame Thouret and Madame Piedcourt, whose age and infirmities required care; Madame Brard, whom she undoubtedly loved to keep close to her because of her character; Sister Marie Dufour, a Converse Sister in poor health; and the Extern Thérèse Soiron.

A second group was settled on 14 *Rue de la Liberté*, now *Rue des Cordeliers*, in a house belonging to Mr. de la Vallée, who occupied the front part facing the street. At the end of a

---

1 [TN] A title indicating the lady in question was a widow, "*veuve*" meaning widow.

courtyard that was longer than it was wide, with flower beds and a well, stood a small building comprising a bakery on the ground floor, a large room and a back room on the first floor, and an attic above. This very modest domicile has not changed in appearance. It had the dual advantage of being sheltered from the noises of the street and the prying eyes of passersby. I visited it: the poor people who live there reported that Mass was once said there, "when there was no longer a church;" in other words, when the churches were closed. Does this tradition not agree with the stay of the Carmelites there? Madame Brideau, Sub-Prioress, was accompanied by Madame Hanisset, Madame d'Hangest, and Catherine Soiron, Extern.

The other two groups lived on 8 *Rue des Boucheries,* now *Rue Neuve,* in the same house but in two separate parts. One of these dwellings had two rooms on the first floor facing the street; a small attic opposite, facing the courtyard; several attic rooms with sloping ceilings above, with a shed in the courtyard: it belonged to a certain Sir Chevalier. We have no information about the other residence. One of these groups was composed of Mesdames Pelras, Trézel, Legros, and Jourdain, along with Sister Roussel, a Converse Sister. The other was composed of Mesdames Chrétien and Philippe, Sister Vérolot, a Converse Sister, and Sister Constance, a Novice. Mother Henriette of Jesus, née de Croissy, was the head of this group. "It was," said Sister Marie of the Incarnation, "a consolation for the incomparable Mother Henriette to have her novices with her," that is to say, those who had done their novitiate under her direction.

The Sister speaks of these four houses as "situated in different quarters of the city." Quite the contrary, they were located in the same quarter, all being close to the Church of Saint-Antoine, very nearby to each other. It is easy to see this, even today, because they still exist, and except for the one on *Rue Saint-Antoine,* which has undergone minor changes, the others have remained in the same condition. Communication was therefore easy, as was the transportation of the food prepared in the house occupied by the Mother Prioress, and the meetings which were held there in the evening. The pastor of the parish, Thibaux, had taken the oath, but he was nonetheless accommodating to the Carmelites: he granted them the use of a special chapel in his church and allowed their chaplain, Abbé Courouble, the faculty to say Mass there, at which they assisted. Thus, the separation of the groups, however real it was, was mitigated. In each house, devotional exercises were carried out with the same order and regularity as in the monastery. Nevertheless, this separation caused many inconveniences, if only because of the cramped living quarters, a slight mortification in comparison with so many others.

The Carmelites had barely been settled in their poor asylums for a few days when, on September 19, around eight o'clock in the evening, the mayor, Mr. de Cayrol, accompanied by de Mosnier, the town prosecutor, arrived at the residence of the Mother Prioress on *Rue Saint-Antoine* and requested her to summon all her Sisters. When they were gathered together, Mr. de Cayrol reminded them that, under the terms of the decree of that past August 14, all people receiving a pension from the State were required to take the oath of liberty and equality. Taking a register from the hand of the town prosecutor, he presented it to the Sisters for their signatures. "We do not come," he added, "with hostile intentions, but simply to ensure your tranquility as well as our own." The Mother Prioress was not ignorant that both Monsieur Emery, Vicar General of Paris, and the delegates of Monsieur de Juigné considered this oath to be lawful. Mr. Rigaud had hastened to inform her of this in order to allay her scruples; even the chaplain, Abbé Courouble, had signed the register that same day. However, the Nuns seemed to remain rather unwilling to take the oath, preferring to wait for a pronouncement from the Pope, or at least to have some time of delay before making a decision.

Thus, the Mother Superior hesitated, all the more so since the sheet of paper, at the bottom of which the mayor invited her to sign, was blank and bore no writing. She pointed this out to the mayor, adding that, if this was about the oath, she was authorized to declare, in the name of her Sisters, that they were not at all willing to lend themselves to this subterfuge. "You are quite wrong to torment yourself so much," replied Mr. de Cayrol. "There is no question of an oath, and you must understand well that the signature you are being asked to provide is an assurance that you will do nothing to disturb the public peace and that, on the contrary, you will do all the good that is in your power. In good faith, do you find that there is anything here to alarm your conscience? So please calm down, and come sign, because I am pressed for time."

Upon these assurances, and confident in the trustworthiness of Mr. de Cayrol, the Mother Prioress signed, followed by her Sisters. Indeed, the register, which still exists, reads: "On Wednesday, September 19, 1792, the ladies presented themselves, etc. (their names follow), formerly Carmelite Nuns, and the lady Marie Placide Langlois, formerly a Benedictine Nun at Royal-Lieu,[2] all citizens of this city, for the purpose of taking the oath prescribed by law, and, consequently, Sir Mosnier, the town prosecutor, read the oath to be loyal to the nation, to uphold liberty and equality, or to die defending them: the aforementioned ladies, with their hands raised, all individually pronounced: *I swear,* and signed, except for Marie Dufour, who declared that she could

2 Baptized on August 6, 1722; professed at the Benedictine monastery of Royal-Lieu at the age of 18, on August 18, 1740, under the religious name of Sister of Saint-Joseph; she was bursar when the house was closed on February 21, 1792. In a rather strange confusion, Madame Campan claims that Madame de Soulanges, the Abbess of Royal-Lieu, and her many Sisters were led to the scaffold on the same day, and that on the carts they sang the *Veni Creator.* However, none of the Benedictines of Royal-Lieu were condemned by the Revolutionary Tribunal of Paris; Madame Campan mistakenly applied to them the tradition relating to the Carmelites. Cf. *Mémoires de Madame Campan* (*Memoirs of Madame Campan*), Didot edition, p. 52, *n.*

not write." This official document does not expressly mention that the Carmelites appeared at the town hall, and in her account, Sister Marie of the Incarnation, an eyewitness, does not say that they went there either. Therefore, it is reasonable to assume that Mr. de Cayrol, out of kindness to the Nuns, wanted to spare them the trip, and especially a walk through the streets of the city, with the more or less derogatory remarks they might have been subjected to, and waiting in the municipal offices. That is why he urged them to sign that very evening; Mosnier signed with them, and the next day, the town clerk added the above formulas.

Did Mr. de Cayrol, who perhaps doubted the success of his endeavor before undertaking it, subsequently boast of having obtained these signatures? Did he not brag a little too much about his cleverness, to the point of suggesting that he had resorted to subterfuge? Sister Marie of the Incarnation stated that the Mother Prioress, Mother Henriette, and herself, having been warned of these rumors, wanted to protest immediately, but that the people who had warned them had pointed out to the Mother Prioress the serious disadvantages that could result from such an untimely complaint, so she decided to delay it. In reality, as the most serious-minded people readily acknowledge, the Mother Prioress had acted prudently in signing and having her Sisters sign. She not only secured the maintenance of their pensions which were much needed in the state of dispossession to which they had been reduced (though, this consideration would not have deterred her if she had believed it to be out of self-interest), but above all, she benefited by not making herself unnecessarily suspect and by ensuring herself tranquility. For his part, the mayor spared himself the trouble of having to take action against Nuns whom he respected. And, in fact, we should note at this point: for twenty-one months, the Carmelites will not be troubled. Did they not owe this to those signatures?[3]

3 Sister Marie of the Incarnation places this scene "perhaps two months after being expelled from the monastery," which would place it around

The necessities to set up in four houses, the novelty of the new routines, and the difficulty of reconciling the common exercises with the division of dwellings had, understandably, caused some disruption to religious regularity. One day, Madame Brideau, the Sub-Prioress, who occupied the house of *Rue des Cordeliers*, arrived at *Rue Saint-Antoine* to speak to the Mother Prioress, but was unable to reach her. As a meticulous observer of the Rule, she must have felt some annoyance and expressed it. In this regard, the Mother Prioress had the following letter delivered to her by the Mother [Thérèse] of the Heart of Mary (Madame Hanisset), who lived with Madame Brideau. It was dated October 1.

> " J. M. J. T .[4]
>
> "If our little Mother *Soup.*[5] was upset by her visit yesterday, I was no less upset by all the obstacles that prevented me from the pleasure that I would have had of responding to a daughter tenderly beloved in Our Lord...but we are neither in the time nor the place to seek satisfactions. To renounce them perpetually and to attach ourselves only to the charitable support of our neighbor for the love of God, which we must always consider in everything, ought to be our daily exercise. He will supplement for you, my very dear Sister and beloved daughter, for all the other exterior practices of mortification that you will absolutely abandon during this month. For such a course of action I wholeheartedly approve and bless with all my heart, the resolution you have decided upon to bring more order to your conduct, which, necessarily, must have strayed from it in these early days, and surely without offending Him whose Will, always adorable and holy, has permitted the sad circumstances that which have caused this disturbance...Let us therefore resume our recollection, prayer, and silence as much

---

mid-November. If this had been the case, how could Madame d'Hangest, who as we shall see, died on October 31, have signed, as can be seen? Therefore, it is necessary to stick to the date given in the register, that is to say, September 19, 1792.

4 Jesus, Mary, Joseph, Teresa [of Avila]. – [TN] Carmelites traditionally write their letters with these initials on the top heading.

5 Probably: "*Sous-prieure;*" (Sub-Prioress), that is to say, Madame Brideau.

> as will be possible at the times when we observed them, as well as our readings. Many persons do not doubt that we are continuing these kinds of exercises and even the same *horarium*: I was struck by their caution not to thus disturb us, and others seemed surprised to see us working at five o'clock and not finding us engaged in some exercise[6]...; Let us therefore do our best, both for the edification of others and for our own benefit...But all this should be done as much as we are able and without scruple, for it is certain that our current situation involves exceptions that an honest heart ought to admit, but which a faithful heart does not abuse...Farewell, then, my very dear daughter, be faithful and peaceful. You will find, in the Heart of Jesus, the heart of a tender mother."

I could have summarized this letter, but I preferred to quote it in its entirety to show with what common sense the Mother Superior, in the new living conditions imposed on her Nuns, knew how to dispense with the secondary requirements of the Rule while ensuring that they carefully preserved its spirit.

On October 31, death took Madame d'Hangest (Marie-Josèphe), Mother Pierre of Jesus. Born in 1742, professed in 1762, she had just turned fifty years old. On August 6, 1790, she had declared that "if she had a thousand lives, she would consecrate them to the state she had embraced, and that nothing could persuade her to leave the house she inhabited, and where she had found happiness." The trials that the Community had since endured hastened the end of this Nun: she died in the house at 14 *Rue des Cordeliers*.

A few weeks later, the Carmelites experienced one of the most serious sorrows that could befall them in their religious life.

The decree, the law of August 26, 1792, which ordered the deportation of any priest receiving a pension who had not taken the schismatic oath to the Civil Constitution of the Clergy, subjected other secular and regular ecclesiastics to the same

6 [TN] In either a communal or a spiritual exercise like mental prayer, spiritual reading, etc.

punishment, even though they were not subject to the oath, if, through certain external acts, they had caused disturbances that had come to the attention of the administrative authorities, or when their removal was requested by six citizens residing in the same department (art. 6). It is always easy to assume that disturbances have occurred; but as for finding six citizens in an entire department to make a denunciation, all it takes is a little willingness.

Two priests from Compiègne, who had taken the oath of liberty and equality but not the schismatic oath of 1790,[7] thus continued to minister their spiritual care: one, Abbé Carlet, to the Sisters of the Visitation, and the other, Abbé Courouble, whom we already know, to the Carmelites. There were six citizens in the city[8] who demanded the deportation of these two priests, not because of any disturbance they had caused, but "in order to prevent any trouble they *might* cause by their conduct."

This denunciation, dated November 20, was the object of a deliberation of the Municipal Council on the 21st, who forwarded it with their approval to the district administrators. Under the terms of the law (Art. 7), the district administrators did not even have the right to deliberate about it; they were

7 [EN] The Oath to the Civil Constitution of the Clergy, which included a clause that made the Church of France unlawfully independent from Rome, was condemned as schismatic by Pope Pius VI in 1791. The Oath of Liberty and Equality, however, was not condemned by the Pope. It was issued in 1792 after the abolition of monarchy, and consisted in the following declaration: "*I swear to be loyal to the nation, and to uphold liberty and equality, or to die defending them.*" As mentioned previously by Victor Pierre, this oath was considered by several priests – including some who were very hostile to the Revolution, such as Fr. Augustin Barruel – as being licit, for one could give a Christian interpretation to liberty and equality. Others believed the words "nation," "liberty" and "equality" were carrying such an Anti-Christian meaning in this context that one could not safely take the oath; among those were Blessed Noël Pinot. See *Life of Blessed Noël Pinot,* translated and published by Shield of Faith Press.

8 Their names were: Duflos, Etave, Guy, Renault, Leclerc Jr., and Capeaumont.

obliged to passively execute the order of the municipality. They justified the measure imposed on these priests as follows: "Considering that the unfavorable opinion that has been conceived against the citizens Carlet and Courouble... may lead to disastrous consequences for themselves, for the former Nuns whose spiritual guidance they continue to provide, and, consequently, for the entire city, and that it is the duty of the administration to prevent disorder of any kind..." (November 23). These strange motives were sufficient to drive the French priests from their country, whose only offense was the peaceful exercise of their ministry.

In virtue of these decrees, the Abbés Carlet and Courouble left Compiègne. Abbé Courouble retired to Germany, where he died in 1800.

The blow that struck their chaplain must have been, in view of the circumstances, particularly significant for the Carmelites. Not only was their priest taken away, the director to whom their consciences had long been accustomed, but how could he be replaced? What appeal could his successor have, given the similar risks he would face! Where could priests even be found in this time of general deportation! Thus, from then on, there was no longer any hope of them being ministered to regularly; and, such occasional ministry would be rare, intermittent, and shrouded in mystery. As a consequence, the freedom of the Nuns was attacked, even in the most intimate sphere. Henceforth, there would be no more public worship, no more Mass at the Church of Saint-Antoine, and no more worship even within their homes, as it would be very difficult to recruit priests who would do so: such were the prospects that lay ahead.

It is understandable that, faced with this brutal suppression of the religious congregations and their prohibition for the future, some families were saying it was necessary that, at least for a time, to go with the flow, and tried to bring back to their homes, where they would be less at risk, their daughters and relatives who had entered religious life in more favorable times. These attempts were unsuccessful and met with firmness and steadfast resolve. In Compiègne, the brother, or at least the cousin of Madame Trézel, took steps to get the Carmelite Nun to renounce the company of her Sisters. Not only did she refuse, but she visited her relative only once, on the occasion of the death of a child baptized the day before, and this visit took place only at the formal invitation of the Prioress. However, this resistance is understandable: for, as we shall see later, the Trézel Family was no less hostile to religion itself than to religious profession.

It was quite different for the mother and the sister of Madame Chrétien, who, retired to their estate near Gisors, insisted that she come and share their refuge. As frightened as she was by the bloody threats that the future held, she did not give in to the wishes of her relatives: "We are," she wrote, "the victims of the world, and we ought to sacrifice ourselves for its reconciliation with God. An eternity of happiness awaits me! Let us hasten, then, let us run toward this end, and let us suffer willingly during the short moments of this life. Today, the storm is raging, but tomorrow we will be in the harbor[9]."

Sister Constance, still a Novice, would have fulfilled the wishes of her parents by returning to them at Saint-Denis; the Soiron sisters, Externs, would have been received into the home of their father, a turner, who lived in Compiègne. The Novice was not bound by profession; and the Externs even less so. The event that could have detached them from the community was the one that bound them to it. As if leaving the cloister had changed nothing for them, all three entrusted their souls, their fate, and their hopes to the destiny of the Carmelites. At this point, they were so closely identified with them that they can no longer be distinguished. They were not Carmelites by the express vows of religion, but they became so by a spontaneous and persevering adherence, and, as they willingly shared the trials of their Sisters, they will not be separated from them in their glory.

9 Account of Sister Marie of the Incarnation, M. S.

Faced with such firm and unanimous resolutions, could the Mother Prioress have continued to conceal her personal aspirations and delay relating them to her community? "The departure from our cloisters," recounted Sister Marie of the Incarnation, "did not change her way of life. On the contrary, she saw in the evils that were devastating the Church and France new reasons to add, if possible, to her works of mortification. She was often pleased to set before our eyes the goal that our Holy Mother Teresa proposed for herself with her reform" (that is to say, that the Carmelites ought to atone and offer their lives for the salvation of France; for this great Saint thought not only of Spain, her homeland, but also of our country, France, which was torn at that time by so many civil and religious struggles, when the faith of the nation was so directly at stake), "and she confessed to us one day that, having meditated on this subject, it had occurred to her to make an act of consecration whereby the Community would offer itself as a holocaust to appease the wrath of God, and so that the divine peace that His beloved Son had come to bring to the world might be restored to the Church and the State. 'It seems to me', she added, 'that since we entered holy religion in order to labor for our own sanctification, that this sacrifice of ourselves should be less costly for us.' Our Mother said an act of consecration: we all promised to join her in it."

However, there was one incident. The two doyennes, Sisters Madame Piedcourt and Madame Thouret (both aged 77), were overcome with emotion, not so much by the sacrifice itself as by the tragic manner in which it was to be carried out: "They could not help expressing to her the fear and trembling that the mere idea of the guillotine caused them. 'Ah! My dear Mother,' they exclaimed, 'do you think...?' And they could not finish, so strong was the impression upon them." Their resistance was a repugnance more physical than moral. "My Sisters," said our Mother, "I do not know what kind of fate awaits us, and although I have confidence that God will give us all the grace to make the sacrifice of our lives for Him, do not think that I am trying to oblige you to join me, and I am not in the least bit upset that you would refuse to do so." Then our good Sisters withdrew; but that very evening they came and threw themselves at the feet of our Mother, asking her forgiveness for the pusillanimity and weakness that they had shown, saying that they, who were at the end of their lives and on the brink of the grave, should be ashamed and blush for this fault, and they asked for the grace that our Mother allow them to join in the act of effective consecration, to which they were faithful until the last day."[10]

This consecration, which Sister Marie of the Incarnation recounted to us as a witness to its circumstances and details, took place "upon leaving our cloisters," and therefore in the last months of the year 1792. It was not a vague and banal act of abandonment to the Will of God, but a formal, express consecration, a renunciation of their life to the extent that a creature can dispose of it: the sacrifice of one's self in order to atone for all. The Mother Prioress could not have thought of imposing it. If she dared to reveal her thoughts, it was because, for her, the dispositions of her Sisters were no longer a mystery. As soon as it was proposed, this consecration was unanimously welcomed as a resolution that was already familiar, long meditated upon and reflected upon: thus, it was irrevocable. Strange in the eyes of the world, Christian mysticism shows its source and example in the sacrifice of the Cross. If Jesus Christ willingly atoned for the sinners of the world, is it not the highest privilege to imitate the Savior by offering our humble lives as a holocaust for our brethren?

This act dominated and characterized the rest of the Carmelites' lives. It was the key to their unwavering cohesion; it was the explanation of their will to remain united, which would prevent them from fleeing the destiny they sensed; of their courage in the midst of suffering; of their joy in sacrifice; of their zeal to die. Others will be victims who are dragged

10 Account of Sister Marie of the Incarnation, M. S. The printed text, pp. 67 and 78-80, offers some variations.

there [to the scaffold], regardless of their courage; but these Nuns will go of their own accord. They offered themselves to God, and two years before undergoing martyrdom, they had wished for and accepted it.

CHAPTER VI

The Missions of Collot d'Herbois and André Dumont (August 1793 – May 1794)

The predictions were accurate. However, the end of that year of 1792, the tragic year of 1793, and even the first months of the year 1794 passed for the Carmelites, if not without sadness, at least without alarm. This tranquility was all the more strange given that Compiègne had not escaped the revolutionary storm any more than other cities. The elections to the Convention had produced some new names: Bourdon (from Oise), Isoré, Anacharsis Cloots, the Prussian, and the intruder Bishop Massieu. In the King's trial, the majority of the elected representatives from Oise (9 out of 12) had voted for death. The municipal elections in the town itself had evidenced an evolution in opinions: while the mayor, Mr. de Cayrol, sought refuge in a position as judge at the District Tribunal, Scellier Jr. was elected to replace him by a unanimity of voters.

These municipal authorities were nothing but figureheads; alongside them, to override or control them, the Convention had just created committees, agents of these popular societies[1]

1 [TN] "Popular societies" were the relative equivalent of a political club, i.e. the meeting, or assembly, of several people, on certain fixed days, to discuss public affairs. The French Revolution led to a significant expansion of these associations, variously called political clubs, popular or patriotic societies, or Jacobin clubs, where citizens discussed political affairs. These societies were modeled on the Jacobin Club in Paris, where some of the "orators" of the era (Robespierre, Danton) "distinguished" themselves. Members debated social issues, commented on current events, and discussed bills put forward by the National Assembly. One of the first clubs to be founded in France was the *Entresol* club, created in Paris in 1720 by Abbés D'Alary and de Saint-Pierre. Concerned by the ideas developed in this club, Cardinal Fleury put an end to its activities in 1731. The first popular societies appeared in 1789 in the major cities of France. Initially, many of them were led by wealthy, reformist notables. They were then called the *Society of Friends of the Constitution*. By 1790, they had proliferated throughout

where revolutionary unrest was brewing. These committees were composed of twelve members elected by society; former nobles and ecclesiastics were excluded. The president was replaced every two weeks; each member received a daily stipend. Initially responsible for policing foreigners, they were later tasked with doing the same for all citizens. The open eye of the Jacobin, framed within the Masonic triangle, was their emblem. They identified suspects and were even given the authority to issue warrants of arrest. At first, they were required to give reasons, but they exempted themselves from this obligation, and the Convention allowed them to do so, except to remind them from time to time to observe the law. An established, recognized, paid institution with legal status, it had a *de facto* power and influence before which the municipalities bowed, willingly or by force. In the political structure, it was a new factor, the importance of which, especially with regard to the Carmelites, the future would reveal. The Revolutionary Committee of Public Safety of Compiègne was composed as follows: Baillet, Bourgeois, Desmarest, a former notary, Nicolas Ducrey, Toussaint Leclerc, an upholsterer, Monnin, Mosnier, a boarding house owner, Potier, Regnard, Rogée, Trézel, and Valansart. Let us refrain from trying to identify each of them more precisely; it is better to leave them in obscurity.

Yet still above them, intended to guide them, train them, and above all protect them from local influences, the Convention had chosen representatives, from among its own members, to send to the departments. They undoubtedly had the mission to expedite mass mobilization, organize provisions, and have weapons manufactured. But, in addition, they were vested

---

France and become important players in local politics. Sometimes, several societies coexisted in the same city. From June 1793 onwards, the societies were purged and the most moderate members were expelled. The popular societies became *revolutionary* . With the Terror, popular society became compulsory. In each city, a popular society, in conjunction with the municipalities and surveillance committees, ensured the proper application of the laws and denounced counter-revolutionaries.

with the right to suspend or dismiss officials, replace them, and even take any measures of general security they deemed necessary, provided that they report it to the Committee of Public Safety within twenty-four hours. Their powers were, *de facto* and *de jure,*[2] unlimited. Thus, Collot d'Herbois, Isoré, Lequinio, and Lejeune were sent to the departments of Oise and Aisne.

We must believe that the municipality, the popular society, and the revolutionary Committee of Compiègne gave complete satisfaction to the representatives of the people: "The public spirit," wrote Collot d'Herbois on August 7, 1793, "is very good in Compiègne. The citizens are preparing a celebration for August 10th that will be truly republican: there will be a cartload of wooden kings that have been unearthed; they will have sacks on their backs, and in those sacks will be all the feudal titles that are to be burned. The cart will be garlanded with all the feudal titles, and the entire tyrannical dynasty will be burned at the foot of the tree of Liberty. The cart itself will also be burned, for, say the patriots, it can serve no purpose after having carried such evil cargo. We rejoice in advance, and this prepared pyre seems to be a sign of the eternal destruction of the plague that will be brought to justice."[3] Such were the republican entertainments prepared by the royal city of Compiègne.

The Law of Suspects[4] had not yet been passed, but it was in preparation, and Collot d'Herbois was already applying it. He had just issued a decree converting the Château of Chantilly into a prison: it was to be put to use. So, under the influence of the proconsul, the revolutionary Committee of Compiègne began deliberations that demonstrated his "very good spirit" and resulted in numerous arrests. The first batch

2 [TN] Both in practice and legally.

3 Aulard: *Les Représentants en mission* (The Representatives on mission), **v.** II, p. 503.

4 [TN] The Law of Suspects (French: *Loi des suspects*) was a decree passed by the French National Convention on 17 September 1793, during the French Revolution that started the Reign of Terror.start of the Reign of Terror.

was on August 25: the general council, in a decision signed by Mayor Scellier Jr. and de Hennequin, the deputy secretary, declared that it "approved and adhered to everything that had been done previously and *would be done in the future.*" They could not have been more docile. Fifty-three signatures accompanied those of the mayor and the secretary.

Among the first victims named were two priests.

The first, Louis-Claude-Germain Collet, aged fifty-eight, was described as "an aristocrat, an apostle of fanaticism, celebrating private Masses." He never attended civic celebrations or primary assemblies; an unsworn priest,[5] celebrating Masses attended by aristocrats and fanatics, chaplain of the chapel of the castle of the former tyrant. Relationships and connections with religious fanatics and former nobles. Insidious character and enemy of the Revolution."[6]

The other priest was Jean-Hippolyte Monache, aged forty-one, formerly a Minim friar, "a fanatic refractory priest who defied the law which prohibited ecclesiastical dress in public. Relationships with fanatics and former Nuns."

Next came the most honorable figures in Compiègne society: Jean-Charles Charmolüe, from a family known in the city for having given several of its daughters to the Carmel since its foundation, was arrested as: "notoriously suspect for never having shown up at the civic celebrations or the primary assemblies, and for never having shown up in the National Guard except when compelled to do so by law."

Mr. Pannelier was accused of "proselytizing." His wife was arrested with him.

Her mother, Marie-Madeleine Bazin, was arrested with her two daughters: "Aristocrats and fanatics. The daughters, victims of the bad influence of their mother, needed to care

5 [TN] A priest who had not taken the schismatic oath.

6 This assessment and the following ones are taken verbatim from the minutes of the revolutionary Committee of Compiègne (Archives of Oise).

for their grandmother, who was worthy of the esteem and pity of all sensitive souls because of her virtues, age, and infirmities. She is in her nineties." These young girls were released shortly afterwards, but their mother remained in prison.

Several members of the Lancry Family were arrested due to being the father, mother, wife, or son of an *émigré*.[7] The father and mother were both in their seventies, and renowned for their "social virtues." The wife had been in a state of dementia since 1787. The two children were aged thirteen and seven.

We should also mention Philippe Le Cornier Jr. and Marie-Françoise-Denise Le Cornier de la Granche, the wife of Le Cornier.

From the middle of August 1793 to October 29, seventy-three residents of Compiègne were arrested and sent in eight convoys to the Chantilly prison by the revolutionary Committee. What a reign of terror for a small town! The only reasons we can see for these arrests are, for the two priests, their priestly fidelity; for certain families, their relation with *émigrés*; for others, their religious beliefs, which were not favorable to the Republic, which made them "aristocrats." Incidentally, those who persecuted them paid tribute to their virtues and testified to the esteem in which they were held.

It is necessary to provide details regarding Mulot de la Ménardière, who, along with his wife, was the subject of similar measures and whose fate would later become intertwined with that of the Carmelites.

The son of a Counselor Secretary to the King, Mulot de la Ménardière lived in Compiègne in the *Faubourg Saint-Germain* in a house that still exists today and is part of the educational establishment of the Sisters of Saint-Joseph of Cluny, now on

7 [EN] The *émigrés* (emigrants) were mostly nobles, sometimes members of the clergy, who had fled to nearby countries (mostly England and the German states) for fear of revolutionary persecutions. The Lancry family was an ancient family of the lower nobility of the Picardie province.

Rue Saint-Joseph. He had no profession. He wrote poetry: the *Affiches de Compiègne et du Beauvaisis*[8] collected his occasional poems, which were insignificant, simple, and utterly talentless. He was then fifty-two years old: neither age nor events of life had cured him of his innocent obsession. He even addressed verses to his wife and published them like the others. Two votes in the elections of May 10, 1791, had named him for mayor of Compiègne — votes cast by whimsical or humorous voters, for he had no interest in politics.

His wife, Marie-Magdeleine-Eléonore Boitel, born in Agnetz near Clermont (Oise), was three years older than him. She had not given him any children. If we are to judge by the similarity of the name, it seems that she must have been related to Madame Boitel, known in religion as Sister [Elisabeth of] Jesus-Mary, who died on February 20, 1791. Her husband was a cousin of Mother Euphrasie, née Brard, so that the Mulot de la Ménardière household was related by a double bond to two Sisters of Carmel. From this arose friendships in which poetry played an ill-fated role.

Within the revolutionary Committee, the name of Mulot did not provoke hostility; he was considered harmless. The same could not be said for his wife, whom one member described as "cranky, mean, and malicious." On August 22, the Committee put them on the agenda; then, at the meeting on the 25th, one member claimed that public opinion considered the couple to be suspect. The Committee immediately ordered the arrest of both of them, on the following grounds: "Mulot and his wife: a scrawny man and a sour woman, suspected of indiscreet remarks, but without evidence in this regard."[9] Nevertheless, they were both imprisoned. After some time, Mulot was released, but his wife was sent to detention in Chantilly on September 27, 1793.

8 [TN] Pieces from Compiègne and Beauvaisis.

9 A later note on Madame Mulot said: "an plotting aristocrat. Her connections with priests and aristocrats. Dangerous character in society." Note dated 6 Germinal, Year II. *Archives of Oise.*

Amidst so many arrests, some of which affected the people and families close to them; while in Senlis, twenty-six Nuns (October 5, 1793) were sent to Chantilly; while in other towns, in the last months of 1793 or the first months of 1794, many others who followed the same kind of life as our Carmelites ended up in prison in order to appear before a Revolutionary Tribunal (and such was, among others, the fate of the Carmelites of the Rue de Grenelle in Paris[10]), our Carmelites of Compiègne were as if forgotten: the storm passed close to them without reaching them.

On December 17, 1793, the two Externs, Catherine and Thérèse Soiron, took the oath of liberty and equality at the municipality. This was undoubtedly done on some secret and benevolent advice, but also with the consent of the Mother Prioress. We can conclude that she did not regret the step she had taken some time before, a step to which she and her companions perhaps owed the tranquility they enjoyed amid the general alarm.

Under the law of 9 Nivôse (December 30, 1793), a new delegation of representatives was tasked with purging the constituted authorities: the operation was to be completed by the 1st of Pluviôse (January 20, 1794). André Dumont, deputy for Somme, succeeded Collot d'Herbois in Oise.

He had only received his commission on 28 Nivôse (January 17). He immediately set out on his campaign. An important and boastful figure, he believed that simply appearing in a town was enough to make everyone tremble before him. On January 20, he wrote from Marat-sur-Oise (the republican name for Compiègne at the time) to the Convention: "Fellow citizens, the ecclesiastical vermin sense that their last hour is approaching. They wanted to rise again, but they have brought about their own downfall. The impostures of these animals have been so thoroughly unmasked, that the citizens

10 [TN] This was not the Carmel of Saint-Denis, but would have been another Carmel in Paris, a little southwest of it. It no longer seems to exist.

of the countryside themselves are helping to empty the former churches. The pews are being used in popular societies and hospitals; the chunks of wood that once were called saints are being used to heat government offices; the niches once termed confessionals are being converted into sentry boxes; the theaters of charlatans, which were called altars and on which priests played with goblets,[11] have been overturned; the pulpits that were used for deception are now used for the publication of laws and the instruction of the people. The churches have been converted into markets, so that people now go to buy their food where for centuries they went to swallow poison."

Such was the style of Pioche Dumont: for, in order to give himself the mask of a revolutionary, he had not failed to exchange his baptismal name of André, whose feast day, in the Gregorian calendar, falls on November 30, for that of *Pioche*,[12] which appeared on the corresponding date of the new calendar (10 Frimaire).

On that same day, at half past five in the evening, citizen Pioche Dumont gathered the citizens of Marat-sur-Oise in order to proceed with the purging of the established authorities: the district administration, municipalities, general council, national officers, civil and commercial courts, surveillance committee, and various other public officials.

The Representative of the People presides. He speaks: roll call is taken. First, the members of the district administration are admitted, except for one who is absent, probably suspect for this reason. From the general council, only one is also rejected. The entire judicial tribunal passes, except for the clerk; the same is true of the commercial tribunal, with the exception of one member. The national officer of the district

11 [EN] In French "*jouer des gobelets*" (play with goblets) could have a double meaning: it might refer to the sacred chalice used during the mass, but the expression itself means cheating, having treacherous and manipulative activities.

12 [TN] "*une pioche*" means a pickaxe.

and that of the commune, admitted to the first trial, are subjected to a second, from which they emerge victorious. The same is true of the revolutionary Committee, in whose honor the second trial, no less favorable than the first, provokes redoubled applause. In summary, out of sixty-nine names submitted to the popular vote, only four were eliminated. In the speech which followed, Pioche Dumont congratulated the citizens of Marat-sur-Oise on the happy trust that reigns between the administrators and the administered.

The rest of the session turned into an idyll: "A young girl of twelve-years intelligently delivered a patriotic speech that was listened to with all the more interest because she did perfect justice to Dumont's virtues and talents." The minutes continued: "The national officer of the district read a patriotic sermon in verse interspersed with songs composed by citizen Perrier, a member of the popular society. He was warmly applauded by the assembly and the representative. The same national officer, on behalf of all the citizens of the district, renewed the sacred oath of the French people and assured Pioche Dumont of their gratitude and attachment. Then, after once again expressing his satisfaction to the citizens of this commune, the representative adjourned the meeting."[13] From such a flattered and applauded representative, from a population where administrators and administered live in such touching harmony, it seems that one could not expect the kind of harsh measures that the Committee of Public Safety might demand.

This Committee exaggerated the "fanaticism" of these departments; Pioche Dumont did not hesitate to tell them so. "Beauvais, 11 Pluviôse (January 30, 1794). I will not hide from you that your concerns pertaining to priests and the fools who listen to them are unfounded for the departments of Oise and Somme. The truth has dispelled the deception, the darkness of the latter cannot obscure the clarity of the

13 National Archives AF, II 162. I quoted the text itself: the Aulard collection only provides an analysis.

former, and the efforts of the ecclesiastical mob would be in vain. If the salvation of the fatherland is as certain as it is that the priests here have been unmasked, we can say: The Republic is saved; or rather: the salvation of the fatherland and the destruction of the priests are both assured." What he says about the department, he also says about Compiègne (16 Ventôse-March 6): "The inhabitants are all equal to the task, and if there are any false brothers, they are well hidden. Republican society is excellent and widely supported; young people receive a fine education; every means is used to ensure that the Revolution is cherished. The Convention is revered, the laws are enforced, and public affairs are going well."[14]

At the end of April, his term of office having come to an end, André Dumont returned to the Convention where, on 17 Messidor (July 5, 1794), he was elected secretary. One of the first, in what appeared to be a complete about-face, he rose up on 9 Thermidor against Robespierre and the Reign of Terror. In fact, he had only served it with words: he put on a show of violence, but stopped short of taking the actions that would have brought it about. He would soon boast of having sent ink when he was asked for blood. Although at the time he uttered these words, they seemed opportunistic and therefore suspect, it is not certain that they were entirely devoid of truth.[15]

During his term, on 3 Germinal (March 23, 1794), the day after the revolutionary Committee of Compiègne sent harsh notes to the Committees of Public Safety and General Security about those of its fellow citizens they had sent to Chantilly, that same Committee granted each of the dispersed Carmelites

---

14 Mon., v. XIX, p. 700. Reprint.

15 He joined the Council of Five Hundred (*Cinq Cents*) in 1795 and left in May 1797. After 18 Brumaire, he was appointed sub-prefect of Abbeville, a position he held until the first Restoration. During the Hundred Days, he was prefect of Pas-de-Calais. When the Bourbons returned for the second time, the law of January 12, 1816, forced him to leave France. He died on October 19, 1836.

a certificate of good citizenship. It therefore had nothing to reproach them for. Two months later (May 17), on the basis of a report sent to them [the Committee of Compiègne] by the Committee of Public Safety that "fanaticism was stirring in the commune," demanding that, "within a week, it be given an exact account of the measures that had been taken to repress the audacity of those who, under the pretext of freedom of worship, dared to foment unrest and stir up movements," the Committee of Compiègne wrote in its minutes: "The Committee immediately hastened to give them the most sincere and truthful account, and to prove to them that Compiègne should not be confused with some of the surrounding communes, which are not yet up to the standards of revolutionary principles and rationale, since it is at an immeasurable distance from fanaticism."

Gibberish, if you will, but an excellent piece of evidence.

CHAPTER VII

TRAVELS

Mothers Le Gros and Jourdain – Sister Marie of the Incarnation – The Mother Prioress

Taking advantage of this security, the Prioress allowed three of her companions to make trips that were, in a sense, necessitated by circumstances.

The brother of Mother Stanislas, née Le Gros, having lost his wife, begged his sister to come and live with him to ease his grief. He lived in Rosières, in the district (*arrondissement*) of Montdidier, a few leagues from Compiègne. It is not the custom in Carmel, even for family reasons, for Sisters to leave the community, even temporarily. But the Carmel of Compiègne was not then in ordinary conditions, and the rigor of the rules or customs could be somewhat relaxed. Moreover, in this circumstance, it was less a matter of gratifying the family than of an act of charity. Her absence was to be temporary and short. One might even wonder if the Mother Prioress did not wish to make clear the freedom she allowed her daughters either to remain together or to dispose of their freedom in another way. She took care, as if to double the ties between the one who was leaving and the community, by assigning her a companion, Madame Jourdain, Mother Thérèse of Jesus, both of whom were already longstanding Nuns and who, on August 5, 1790, like their Sisters, had both firmly declared their intention to live and die as Carmelites. Their well-known sentiments, the length of their Profession, and their age testified that by this absence, they were not seeking to escape either the religious life or the hardships of their community.

When did this departure take place? Sister Marie of the Incarnation says: "in May 1794," but this is an error, because of the two letters that remain from one of the two Sisters to the

Prioress: the first is dated April 6, the second May 6. The first even mentions a letter from the Prioress which, once posted, took ten days to arrive. The separation would therefore date back to the beginning of March 1794.

These two letters from Mother Thérèse bear witness to the close relationship that the two absent members maintained with the Community, to the deep affection they continued to have for their companions and friends in Compiègne, and to the pleasure they took, even while being far from them, in talking about them with their relatives and friends. These letters, which are extremely simple, reveal all the more clearly the feelings and the character of joyful intimacy that reigned among all these souls. On the other hand, there is nothing in them to suggest that these Nuns considered themselves to be anything other than absent.

Here it is Mother Thérèse, née Jourdain, who pens: "We are concerned, dear Mother, about your health," she writes on April 6, "but especially about that of my Sister [Charlotte] of the Resurrection (Madame Thouret, then aged seventy-nine), whom you told me was very ill. Give us news of her and of all our dear Sisters, to whom we say a thousand tender and gracious things more with our hearts than with our mouths. Give us also, dear Mother, news of our good Fathers [probably the priests who ministered to them in Compiègne] and of all of those who are with them. There is not a day that goes by that we do not commend them to the Lord. What has become of our poor *curés?*[1] I am still interested in them despite their deviation; their blindness pains me, and I pray for them every day that they may recognize themselves. Far from condemning them, I have the greatest compassion for them and often apply to myself this passage from Scripture: '*Let him who stands take heed lest he fall.*'"[2] Is it not touching to see such indulgence in those persons whose austerity might

1 An allusion to the curés of Saint-Jacques, Saint-Antoine, and Saint-Germain in Compiègne who had taken the oath and accepted civil functions.

2 *Qui stat videat ne cadat.* St. Paul: 1 Cor. 10:12

have led them to more severe judgments?

She also gives news of Mother Stanislas, who she spares no less effort in the village than at Carmel: "My Sister Stanislas is feeling a little unwell; I think it is only due to the fatigue she has suffered from the laundry we have just done; I am confident that a little rest will restore her completely...Our dear brother is a little tired from the laundry, as he did his fair share, drawing about a hundred buckets of water. He asked me to convey his respects to you, Mother Henriette, and all our dear Sisters."

At that time, one avoided sending letters by post mail: instead, they would seize the opportunity of finding a traveler who could deliver them. "Oh, what joy!" wrote Mother Thérèse on May 6. "Behold, another opportunity has presented itself. I will not let it pass without giving you our news and assuring you of our respectful affection." Between this letter and the previous one, the "dear brother" had returned from Compiègne; they were now expecting friends from Lions: "Oh! how much we will talk about you all; you have no idea, dear Mother, how great an affection they have for you."

Then follows a stream of all the people of Compiègne to whom they wish to convey their regards: these were the Christian friends whom times of trial had bound closer to the Carmelites. She also thinks no less of her Sisters' fears and trials: "We are still very much at peace here, and I wish you could be the same, but that is far from the case when I think of all the anxieties you have been experiencing for so long. I don't know how you can withstand them; the good God supports you all, and I have confidence that He will do so until the end." Finally, in a postscript: "We are very pained by the situation of our dear captives [probably those in Chantilly]. We pray for them daily that God may be their consolation. Adieu once again, dear Mother, I am not able to leave you. A thousand tender greetings to Mother Henriette."

In these letters, so affectionate, so simple, so full of memories of everyone, can we not recognize a soul who has abandoned herself in obedience to the place where she has been placed? Docile to the orders of her Prioress, who allowed her to leave, she would be no less so if it pleased her Mother to call her back.

Around May 16, another absence occurred: Madame Philippe, Sister Marie of the Incarnation, was called to Paris for the liquidation of an annuity from the State. She had counted on only spending a few days there, but the matter dragged on longer. She was sent, as she said, "from Caiaphas to Pilate, and from Pilate to Herod," that is to say, from office to office. In the meantime, she ran errands for her Sisters and friends in Compiègne.

We have seen how, in her correspondence with the Superior of Carmel, Mother Euphrasia reproached herself for feelings of jealousy and pride. She then wrote the following letter to Sister Marie of the Incarnation: "Join with me, my dear good little Sister, in giving thanks to the Lord for what He has done, in His infinite goodness: He has deigned to let fall from my eyes the enormous scales that covered them, and He snatched me from the sight of the awful precipice prepared by that infernal spirit of pride, envy, and jealousy by which I had the misfortune to always allow myself to be led. I should not have been afraid to humble myself, and I can tell you that I have now done so with all the sincerity of my heart. I hope that the Lord, touched by my repentance, will pardon my faults. Since I have recovered my peace of conscience, the guillotine no longer frightens me so much, and I would consider it a blessing of the mercy of my God if He granted me the grace, unworthy as I am, of being assured of the glory of martyrdom." It was to this labor of self-improvement, to this noble ambition of her perfection that she devoted herself: she, the woman whom Queen Marie Leczinska once called her "most amiable philosopher."

In her turn, the Prioress would also be obliged to come to

Paris.

Her mother, now a widow, was thinking of retiring to Ornans (Doubs) to live with the family of her husband. She pressed her daughter to come: "Behold, the Feast of Saint John is approaching," she wrote her, "and everything tells me that there is no time to lose.... Consult your sensitive heart, which will surely not be able to bear seeing a mother full of years move more than 80 leagues away without giving her the consolation she expects from you, nor of having any hope of ever seeing you again. I trust that Our Lord will not oppose my desire, for I never cease to ask Him to fulfill His Holy Will."

However, the Prioress did not budge. Was she afraid that the departures of Sisters Le Gros and Jourdain, whose absence was likely to be prolonged, and then that of Sister Marie of the Incarnation, whose return was also delayed, would cast some doubt in the souls of those who remained? For her part, by leaving herself, would her absence not provide a pretext for some negative interpretations? Was not this even giving too much credence to familial affection, which she had sacrificed by her religious vows? On June 10, her mother, surprised by her delay, wrote to her again: "I am surprised, my dear daughter, that your cousin did not find you at the carriage after sending for you as soon as she received my last letter. Do not imagine that your journey is only for the satisfaction of seeing you; it is absolutely most urgent and therefore very necessary, as I am not able to determine anything in my affairs unless you are present. I was assured of this again when I was at the office of the notary. The time is approaching, leave has been granted, and I am, so to speak, entirely ready to set off on a journey of nearly 100 leagues. As you know, I am 79 years old, which should be reason enough for you to make up your mind. I therefore await your arrival next Friday."

Faced with these appeals of her mother, to which it seems Monsieur Rigaud, the Superior, had added a permission or even an order at the end of April, the Mother Superior made her decision. She left her companions and, no doubt armed with her Certificate of Good Citizenship (it would have been imprudent to neglect this precaution), she took the stagecoach on Friday, June 13. She intended to stay in Paris for only eight days, the time strictly necessary to complete her affairs. She lodged with her mother on *Rue des Prêtres-Saint-Paul*[3].

In the course of her occupations, she undoubtedly had the occasion to talk to Monsieur Rigaud and be informed by him about everything concerning the Carmels. Did she learn how the mothers of the convent on *Rue de Grenelle*, brought before the Revolutionary Tribunal of Paris in February, had been summoned by the president, and even urged by the audience and the gendarmes, to take the oath of liberty and equality? How, having obstinately refused, they had been condemned by this ruler to imprisonment, a lenient punishment for the time? Did she know of the equally energetic responses of her Sisters in Lyon, and of the death on the scaffold of Sister Vial? Or, of that of Madame de Chamboran, a Carmelite of Saint-Denis in Paris, by reason of her correspondence with *émigrés?*[4] And of so many other heroic deaths of Nuns from the other Orders, and so many mass imprisonments in certain cities?

A circumstance, which in Paris was then a daily occurrence, happened to catch her eye and give her one of those subtle warning signs which, though terrible for others, in her case, on the contrary, harmonized with her ordinary desires and thoughts.

As soon as Sister Marie of the Incarnation had learned of

---

3 Today it is the *Rue Charlemagne*, named as such by royal decree on August 5, 1844.

4 Marie-Catherine-Gabrielle de Chamboran was condemned to death and executed on 7 Germinal Year II—March 27, 1794 (Wallon, *Revolutionary Tribunal of Paris*, v. III, p. 78). The Mother Prioress appears to have been aware of this. Another lady from the Chamboran Family (Marie-Rose), widow of Duplessis, was sentenced and executed on 28 Messidor - July 16, 1794, that is, the day before the Carmelites were judged. The two women have sometimes been confused with each other, at least as far as the dates of their executions are concerned.

the arrival of the Mother Prioress in Paris, she hastened to join her. One day, as they were leaving the *Rue des Prêtres-Saint-Paul*, they wanted to cross *Rue Saint-Antoine*, but they were unable to do so because of the large crowd that had gathered there. A tumultuous crowd preceded an escort of guards on horseback. These were the carts of death, which had changed their route a few days earlier. The shopkeepers on *Rue Saint-Honoré* had complained that the daily passage of the horrible procession was hurting their business. So, it was at first diverted to the site where the Bastille formerly stood, then, a few days later, to the *Place du Trône renversé*, now *Place de la Nation*: from June 17 onwards, the scaffold was erected there.

Sister Marie of the Incarnation, who witnessed the scene, recounts it to us: "When I caught a glimpse of the mounted guard," she said, "I urged our Mother that we should retrace our steps, telling her that these were victims being led to their deaths and that every time such a spectacle presented itself to my sight, I thought I myself would die from the shock it caused me. The spirit of faith that animated our Mother caused her to pray and beg me to stay. 'Ah! Do not deny me,' she said, 'the sad consolation of seeing how the saints go to their death.' I was forced to yield to her wishes. Without seeking it, we found ourselves very close to the cart of death. At the moment when they passed in front of us, our Mother seemed enraptured by the serenity that appeared on the faces of the victims. Two of them had their eyes fixed on us, and I said to our Mother, 'Do you not perceive how these men are looking at us? They seem to be saying to us, 'Soon you will follow the same path!'' — 'Ah! What happiness that would be for us,' exclaimed our Mother, 'if God would deign to grant us that grace!'" This thought filled her with joy.

Until that moment, she had only envisaged martyrdom through her mystical desires, as a sacrifice pleasing to God and in accordance, if not with the traditions of Carmel, then at least with the vows of Saint Teresa. On this day, she had a striking spectacle before her: but this crowd, these carts, these guards, all this external display, held her attention less than these recollected men upon the carts, undoubtedly priests (there were some almost every day), who smiled at their impending death and seemed to exhort the witnesses of their sacrifice to courage and prayer. "What a favor," she exclaimed again, "if God found us worthy of such happiness!" But she did not allow her own passion for sacrifice carry her beyond the proper limits: personally devoted as a Nun, yet prudent as a mother is to her daughters, she added: "May God forbid that my desire to die for His love should cause me to commit the slightest imprudence!"

When it came time to part ways with Sister Marie of the Incarnation, she told her that she had learned from a reliable source that Bp. de Bourdeilles, the Bishop of Soissons[5] (to which Compiègne then belonged), condemned the oath of liberty and equality; and that, as for her, she intended to no longer receive her pension. Already, perhaps, in recollecting the memories of so many Nuns, especially Carmelites, who had refused to take this oath before the revolutionary tribunals, the Mother Prioress had felt some scruples arise within her and had resolved to make a prompt retraction at all costs. "I approve of you being here," she said to Sister Marie of the Incarnation, "but let that not prevent you from coming back to us as soon as you are able. May I believe you are as eager as I am to leave the capital, this place of horror and abomination?"

Sister Marie of the Incarnation still had five days to wait before the completion of her affairs. As the Mother Prioress seemed to want her to return with her to Compiègne immediately,

---

5 Henri-Joseph Claude, born December 7, 1720; Bishop of Tulle, 1762-1764; transferred to Soissons. On February 23, 1791, he protested against the usurpation of his seat; the municipality ordered him to leave; his carriage was pursued by the mob he had fed. He retired successively to Brussels, Munster, and Granhof; he resigned in 1801 and died in Paris on December 12, 1802, at the age of 82. He was buried in the Vaugirard cemetery.

only to return to Paris a few days later, she pointed out to her that this return, followed almost immediately by another trip, might appear suspicious: "Ah! If only you would allow me, my dear Mother, to go and spend the five days I still have to wait for my affairs to be settled in Gisors?"

Once permission had been obtained, the two Nuns parted ways, and at the same hour that Sister Marie of the Incarnation left for Gisors, the Mother Prioress set off for Compiègne.

CHAPTER VIII

THE ARREST

4 Messidor Year II – June 22, 1794

On that same day, June 21–3 Messidor, just as the Mother Prioress was boarding the stagecoach to return to Compiègne, the Revolutionary Committee of Public Safety of the city, under the presidency of Mosnier, issued the following decree:

> On receiving news that the former Carmelites, scattered across three or four sections of this commune, are meeting in the evening; and that, since the arrest of the notorious *Théot,* who calls herself *Mother of God,*[1] there appears to be more commotion, and one may perceive greater eagerness on the part of the former Nuns and certain devout women of the commune;
>
> The Committee, considering that there is already a complaint in its records attesting that these ladies still live in community; that they still live under the fanatical regime of their former convent; that there may exist criminal correspondence between these former Nuns and the fanatics of Paris; that there is reason to suspect that they hold meetings driven by fanaticism;
>
> Decrees that the members [of said Committee], divided into several groups, shall visit the various houses occupied by them, and that each group shall be accompanied by a sufficient number of dragoons.

This search took place immediately and simultaneously in all three houses, resulting in the seizure of several papers. In the evening, the Mother Prioress arrived; three or four of her Sisters had come to meet her, to express their joy at her return and to inform her as soon as possible of the incident during

1 [EN] Catherine Théot (1716-1794) was a false mystic who pretended to receive visions about a revolutionary Messias. She was arrested in June 1794 by enemies of Robespierre who thought her case could be evidence of a conspiracy of Robespierre to seize even more power.

the day.

The next morning, after examining the papers, the Committee recognized (at least that is the term it used) "that there was criminal correspondence between the former Carmelites aimed at restoring the monarchy, announcing the desire for counter-revolution, the debasement and even dissolution of the National Convention and the destruction of the Republic." They ordered their immediate arrest, transfer to prison, and the solitary confinement of the Carmelite Nuns living in the Saiget and Chevalier houses, that is to say, those on *Rue de Dampierre* (*Rue Saint-Antoine*) and *Rue des Boucheries* (*Rue Neuve*). The first group consisted of the Prioress, Sisters Thouret and Brard, the Converse Sister, Marie Dufour, and the Extern, Thérèse Soiron. The second group consisted of six persons: Sister Henriette de Croissy with Sisters Trézel and Pelras; two Converse Sisters, Angélique Roussel and Élisabeth Vérolot; and finally the Novice, Constance Meunier. A second, very harsh visit was to follow these arrests, carried out by two members of the Committee, Valansart and Rogée, accompanied by the armed forces.

The Commissioners filed new papers in the office, and the Committee immediately issued a second decree, the terms of which are as follows:

> Having examined these documents, the Committee, considering that the former Nuns, in defiance of the law, although separated into different houses, still lived in community; that they observed the same rules as those of their former monastery, that their correspondence proves that they were secretly plotting against liberty; that their conspiracies had very extensive ramifications; that the citizen Mulot de Laménardière was among the number of their accomplices, sending them anti-revolutionary writings, has decreed:
>
> I. – That the former Carmelite Nuns lodging with the citizen Lavallée, on *Rue de la Liberté*, be immediately arrested and transferred to the prison;
>
> II. – That the citizen Mulot de Laménardière would also be

arrested, transferred to the said prison, and his papers sealed;

III. – That the citizens Valansart, Rogée, and Leclerc would be charged with executing this order.

This third group, living with the Vallée couple on *Rue de la Liberté* (now *Rue des Cordeliers*), included five Nuns: Sister Brideau, Sub-Prioress; Sisters Chrétien, Hanisset, and Piedcourt; and Catherine Soiron, the Extern. At the beginning of their dispersion, there had been four groups, but since then, the death of Madame d'Hangest and the prolonged absence of Sisters Jourdain and Legros had reduced them to three. Sister Marie of the Incarnation was still in Paris.

When this last group of Sisters was torn from their home, the Sub-Prioress, Madame Brideau, said to Monsieur and Madame de la Vallée, the owners: "We leave you everything we have; if we return, you will give it all back to us; if we do not return, you will keep it in memory of us and as a token of our gratitude for all the kindness you have shown us." This is what Monsieur de Bussière, her grandson, recounts as a tradition he had heard from the mouth of his grandmother, who was present at the time (she was eighteen years old).[2] He adds: "There were, in fact, in the house, and especially in the apartment of my family, a fairly large number of objects belonging to the Nuns. All those things in the room occupied by them were mercilessly broken. Among these broken objects, I will mention, in particular, a tabernacle for the altar and a prie-dieu arranged in the form of an oratory. When the tabernacle was smashed to pieces, one of the *sans-culottes*[3] kicked the debris toward the young girl, who was my grandmother, saying to her: 'Citizen, here's something to

2 Ch. Marie Onésime Bussière de Nercy de Vestu, born September 2, 1830, former registrar (*Trial of the Ordinary*) **vol**. I, p. 449.

3 [TN] In the French Revolution, the "sans-culottes" *(without "culottes")* were the radical left-wing partisans of the lower classes; typically urban laborers, which dominated France. These popular protesters wore striped trousers instead of breeches (i.e. culottes), a symbol of the old regime's *(Ancien Régime)* aristocrats and bourgeoisie.

make a doghouse for your dog.' As for the small oratory, it contained three statues: the Child Jesus, the Blessed Virgin, and Saint Joseph. These three statues were broken, but their heads were saved by the piety of my grandmother." Most of these objects, or rather relics, later returned to the Carmelites of Compiègne and of Meaux.

Under an escort of dragoons, and undoubtedly all together, the Carmelites were conducted to the former convent of Sainte-Marie of the Visitation on *Rue des Minimes*. After its having been used to lodge soldiers passing through, it had become, like so many other convents, a prison. Collot d'Herbois had populated it in August and September 1793 with suspects from Compiègne, who were gradually evacuated to Chantilly. On October 23, 1793, twenty-one English Benedictines – fifteen Nuns and six Converse Sisters – accompanied by two chaplains, were brought there from Cambrai. Their Order, forced to leave England due to Protestant intolerance, had continued in Cambrai since 1623, like so many English, Irish, and Scottish Monks, Nuns, and Priests who, for the same reasons and under the same conditions, had taken refuge in France and lived in Paris, Douai, Saint-Omer, and Bordeaux, protected not only by Catholic hospitality but also by treatises.

An Austrian army approached Cambrai to lay siege to it, so the Nuns were hastily expelled, either because they were Nuns or because they were English. On October 18, while a band of armed men surrounded their convent, another group entered, pillaged at will, and expelled the Nuns without allowing them to take any provisions or belongings with them. They were thrown onto open carts, insulted as they passed, and, between a double line of dragoons, they traveled for five days and finally arrived in Compiègne, where they were lodged at the Visitation, in the rooms of the infirmary.

The winter of 1793-1794 was very difficult for them. They were left without heat, with almost no bread or very little of it, and of very poor quality. They engaged in needlework and other crafts, which provided very little to meet their needs.

Illness, suffering, and extreme deprivation claimed their victims: their venerable chaplain, Dom Augustine Walher, president or Abbot General of the English Benedictine Congregation, whose learning and piety had made him dear to Pius VI, died on January 13, 1794; the next day, the 14th, one of the Nuns died; on the 21st, a second; on February 6th, a third; and, at the end of March, a fourth. They were reduced to seventeen. Reverend James Higginson, recently given to Dom Walher as an assistant chaplain, was in prison with the Nuns, but was not allowed to see them.

The Carmelites were placed in the rooms opposite those of the English Benedictines; but to separate them completely, the windows were nailed shut and a wall was even built. They were therefore neighbors, but not companions in the prison. The Prioress, Dame Anna Blyde, stated in a letter that she saw the Carmelites only twice, and even then surreptitiously, *"though with great fear."*[4]

Mulot de la Ménardière was also an inmate at the Visitation in another part of the building.

4 Cf. *A brief narrative of the seizure of the Benedictine Dames of Cambray, of their sufferings while in the hands of the French Republicans, and of their arrival in England. By one of the Religious who was an eyewitness to the events she relates. Signed: Ann Teresa Partington* (Written in 1795 or 1796). The author of this account was one of the imprisoned Benedictines; a very valuable and touching testimony.

CHAPTER IX

THE SEIZED DOCUMENTS

To which causes can we attribute this almost unexpected resurgence of severity? How is it that the Revolutionary Committee of Compiègne, which until then had been so tolerant and even indifferent towards the Carmelites, suddenly became concerned about their existence and their way of life? How did they come to accuse them of ridiculous plots aimed at destroying the Convention and annihilating the Republic?

First, there are the general causes: the law of 27 Germinal Year II—April 16, 1794, which abolished the military tribunals and commissions in the departments, brought all suspects from all parts of the country to Paris, and gathered them all before the Committee of Public Safety. Then there was the law of 22 Prairial—June 10, 1794, which recognized only one crime: conspiracy; only one punishment: death; only one type of evidence: the conscience of the jurors; and admitted no laws, no witnesses, and no defense. Denunciations filled the prisons: the Revolutionary Tribunal, freed from all procedure, emptied them.

Under pressure from this arbitrary legislation, revolutionary committees found themselves caught between two extremes: either to not denounce anyone and make themselves suspect, or to resign themselves to doing so in order to avoid being accused of being soft. But while it cost them dearly to crack down on their fellow citizens, neighbors, and friends, they were also very embarrassed to find a reason for denouncing them. In a city where, as they themselves said, a "very good spirit" reigned, how could they uncover conspirators? Nevertheless, these committees met regularly; every two weeks they changed their president and secretary; the meetings had to be kept busy. Individually, each member was perhaps harmless; but when they got together, either because of the momentum of numbers, or so as not to appear inactive, they would make a decision on a risky motion that no one dared to contradict, without having weighed the consequences.

We believe that the following incident had an influence on the sudden initiative taken by the revolutionary Committee of Compiègne with regard to the Carmelites, and upon the definition they applied to their alleged crimes.

A few days earlier (27 Prairial—June 17), Vadier, a member of the Committee of Public Safety, had denounced from the pulpit of the Convention the conspiracy of "bigots" and "simpletons," pseudo-scholars, and Mesmerists, whose leader and 'priestess' was Catherine Théot, who called herself the *'Mother of God.'* He ridiculed them, but he denounced them nonetheless as agents of conspiracy. Above all, he did not fail to link them to priests of all countries and all religions. "When," he said, "crucifixes, Sacred Hearts, and rosaries are the rallying signs of the conspirators; when they are found in the pockets of *émigrés*, on the chests of the brigands of the Vendée, and when we see these sinister emblems in the garrets of the alleged *'Mother of God'*... can you calmly and without concern watch a centre of fanaticism, a madhouse, and a nursery of Cordays form around the National Assembly?"[1] He also reported alleged royalist connections, links with *émigrés*, a full-length portrait of the young "Capet,"[2] and demanded that Catherine Théot and her accomplices be brought before the revolutionary Tribunal on charges of conspiracy.

Catherine Théot! To equate the pitiful theosophist with the Carmelites — what an aberration, or rather, what nonsense! The ingenious committee of Compiègne fell for it; it linked

1 Allusion to Charlotte Corday who, on July 13, 1793, assassinated Marat, *the Friend of the people.*

2 [EN] After the abolition of the monarchy, the French royal family, who were to be considered as "normal citizens," were referred to as "Capet," based on the nickname of the founder of the dynasty, Hughes Capet (reigned 987-996). — Here the "young Capet" was Louis XVII, the son of Louis XVI, who died in prison in 1795 at age 10.

the cause of the Carmelites to that of the alleged *'Mother of God'*, supposing a connection, an alliance, and a criminal correspondence between the former Nuns and the fanatics of Paris. None of the seized documents supported this strange connection: it was only a first impression, or, if you will, a pretext, hastily seized upon. They did not persist in maintaining the pretext, but they did not renounce the arrest.

Many papers and objects were seized: let us examine them in detail.

There are two sets of documents. The first consists of letters of spiritual direction or other private correspondence, which the Committee immediately dismissed and with which we need not concern ourselves; this set is now in the Oise archives. The second will form the case file: it is kept in the National Archives, among the papers of the revolutionary Tribunal of Paris.

Most of the letters are addressed to the Prioress. Some date back to 1790. One is from a Nun asking to associate the Carmel of Compiègne with a prayer league, a universal novena "for the time of calamities in which we find ourselves." Another, from an Abbé Chomel, a close friend of the Lidoine family, laments the plunderings of which the Church was victim. His letter ends with these lines, which, at that date (1790), seem prophetic: "In these stormy times, we must prepare ourselves for martyrdom, for, according to all appearances, that is where we will end up. Blessed are those who merit to receive the crown!" The Prioress was worthy of understanding these words.

In 1791, the Nuns were concerned not so much about the oath itself as about the dealings they risked having with intruder bishops or juror priests. One of them, from the Presentation convent of Senlis, wrote (April 1791): "The bishop (Massieu) is the greatest object of our fears; we do not intend to ring our bells, as we have no intention of recognizing him. We do not know what will happen." This seditious thought was underlined by the public prosecutor with a pencil stroke.

An Ursuline Nun in Paris dreaded the arrival of Gobel, the intruder bishop, and explained the reception she was preparing for him (July 6, 1791): it was quite a procedure. "We do not know, Madame, how our Sisters, the Ursulines of Beauvais, are behaving towards Monsieur Massieu, but we can tell you with certainty that, in this capital, we are all determined not to recognize the intruder in any way. If he were to visit this house and ask to enter, we would refuse to open the door to him; if he insisted and threatened, we would open the door to avoid a greater scandal caused by violence, but we would not take him to the church; he would go alone if he wanted to. If he asked to see our registers, as a legitimate bishop making his visit, we would not show them to him. If he absolutely insisted on seeing them, we would show them to him, telling him that we were not showing them to him in recognition of him as our bishop, but to avoid violence, for we recognize no other bishop than Bishop de Juigné. After he would leave, we would have a report drawn up stating that Monsieur so-and-so had come to be recognized, that he had entered by force, and, in short, that we did not recognize him, and that all the acts he had performed in our house were acts of violence. The superior and the older Nuns would sign this report drawn up by a notary, and this report would be preserved...."

The following unsigned note, whose handwriting and author are unknown to us, must undoubtedly also be attributed to the year 1791.[3] "You shall add to your general intentions for the needs of the Church and the State, that those members who form the districts and municipalities may *obtain* the light to know *all the evil they do by lending themselves* to the execution *of decrees contrary to Religion*, and to have the fidelity *to refuse them even at the risk of their lives or*

3 We find it impossible to recognize the handwriting of Abbé Rigaud here, or, even more so that of Mulot de la Ménardière, who had no business interfering in such spiritual matters.

to renounce absolutely any employment that cannot be reconciled with Christianity." From these repeated emphases, it is clear that fidelity to the [Catholic] Religion and the scruples[4] that followed from it, struck the authorities reading these things as an offense against the revolutionary government.

A woodcut depicting Louis XVI in bust form with the following poor verses beneath it was seized from the Mother Superior:

Of our freedom, he is the renovator,

Of Nestor, of Titus, the august imitator.

What am I saying? O people blessed by his extreme love,

You can only compare this great King to himself.[5]

— P. de Berainville.

Written in 1791, and entirely constitutional at that date, these verses and this portrait ceased to be so on August 10, 1792.

Similarly, an accusatory bracket enclosed a passage from a letter written by a Nun from Senlis who lamented the death of the King and praised his testament and his resignation: "He never showed himself more worthy of reigning than when they wanted to destroy him. I never cease to be amazed, and I cannot conceive how anyone could have been hard-hearted enough to condemn him to death. However, God has allowed it, and I do not wish to meddle in these designs." For someone who "murmurs and is surprised," it must be said that she resigned herself quickly and was far from rebelling. "Today (March 7, 1793)," she writes further on, and this passage is also underlined, "it is said that the Austrians forced the French patriots to lift the siege of Maastricht and that the

4 [EN] i.e. not in the sense of an unreasonable scruple, but a careful attention not to violate one's conscience.

5 [TN] *De notre liberté, c'est le restaurateur, / Des Nestor, des Titus auguste imitateur. / Que dis-je? O peuple heureux par son amour extrême, / Tu ne peux comparer ce grand Roi qu'à lui-même.*

6,000 *émigrés* who were there defended it. May God allow all this to succeed for a greater good! For my part, I hope that we may serve Him more freely than at present, and that I may atone for all my infidelities in the depths of a cloister!" A modest wish, we must admit, from such a Nun driven from her cloister who asks only for the freedom to return to it.

A relic of Madame Acarie, which the Mother Prioress had brought back from Paris; a hymn to the Sacred Heart, obviously composed for Nuns,[6] by Abbé D..., formerly a priest at the parish of Saint-Sulpice in Paris; and finally, some images of the Sacred Heart, complete the group of items entered into the official record as incriminating evidence. Admittedly, the result of the seizure was mediocre and insignificant, but let us remember Vadier's allusions to crucifixes, Sacred Hearts, and rosaries, which he denounced as "the rallying signs of the conspirators." Did passionate, prejudiced minds, who were embarrassed to identify conspiracies that had to be invented, not feel relieved of their concerns when they discovered similar signs among a group of Nuns whom they did not know how to accuse?

A series of five pieces of evidence were gratuitously attributed to this average and harmless character we mentioned earlier, Mulot de la Ménardière. These pieces were, moreover, utterly insignificant in themselves, or completely unrelated to the man they were supposed to concern.

He loved to rhyme, as we know. Poor rhymester!

It must have been in 1792, during the parliamentary disputes over the *veto* that the king had imposed on several decrees passed by the Assembly. Mother Euphrasie wrote

---

6 This was, according to the indictment, "the battle cry of the Vendée rebels." But how could soldiers be expected to relate to the following verses: "Sacred Heart of a God who loves us... nothing in this lonely cloister"; or: "Like a timid dove, I come to you seeking peace"; or again: "Behold, above all, O gentle Heart, Behold these virgins who, night and day, Fan the sacred fire of Thy Love in Thy sanctuary?" – Moreover, in 1791, was there even a Vendée?

to her cousin that, due to the rain and cold, Providence had *vetoed* her work in the garden. This word "*veto*" inspired the "muse" of her cousin, and he replied:

The veto of our grand master
Is a very comforting veto.
The flowers, the buds ready to bloom,
Foretold us of their nullity.
He makes them even more beautiful;
He suspends their nativity.

Until then, nothing but innocence. Here are the incriminating verses:

The cold will destroy the insects;
If only it would destroy all the wicked;
All the Jacobin sects,
And a number of the representatives!
This wish comes from my desire
To see happiness reborn;
To see my homeland happy;
It is the desire of all my heart.

Such is, in verses that the reader will appreciate as being remarkably dull, the only piece for which Mulot can be criticized.

Next comes a note addressed to his cousin in June or July 1793, when she was living at the Saiget house on *Rue de Dampierre*, informing her that «the good and sensitive friend he was expecting from Paris has just arrived and that he is expecting her the next day, around ten or ten-thirty, Madame the Superior with whichever of her ladies she wishes, and, of course, her cousin." Was this not Monsieur Rigaud, who had come from Paris to see his dear Carmelites and preferred to see them in the third house? This is what will be imputed against Mulot as a "fanatical gathering."

The third piece of evidence is not by Mulot, but by his sister. It is dated July 22, 1792, that is to say, the day of the feast of Madame Mulot (Saint Madeleine).[7] She wishes her sister-in-law a happy name day and congratulates Mulot on the verses he has written for his wife on this occasion. Here, she does not hesitate to speak of "the volunteers,[8] who are all lazy, vagabonds, impious and without manners, and majority of them, commoners and even the scum of society, without feelings, without hearts, without character, with no other God than their vagabond life, their passions and their bellies." One can well imagine that this all-too-accurate portrait was angrily penned, as was this other passage: "Let us pity the wicked and tremble at the just punishment they deserve. Let us pray to God that they may be converted; hats and bonnets the color of blood have always revolted me." Who wrote this letter? It was not Mulot: his only fault was to receive it and, in those times of inquisition, to keep it.

The following two pieces do not apply to him.

A Nun from Senlis, Sister Saint John the Evangelist, born Madeleine Prévost, wrote to the Mother Prioress in 1791 or 1792: "Never hesitate to write to my father when you need to; I will make sure he receives it. But, between you and I, my dear Mother, I recommend prudence. People talk too much in Compiègne, and this was told to me in Senlis, from someone influential who told me that people were failing to be circumspect, and that this could have consequences. I was asked to inform him *myself*, so that he could recommend silence, a virtue so necessary! Please tell this to his entire family. His wife is still grieving over the illness in question: you are no doubt aware of the death of her eldest son." This intemperance of speech does not therefore apply to the Nuns,

7 [TN] "Madeleine" is the French name for "Magdalene."

8 [EN] The National Volunteers were people who freely joined the French army between 1791 and 1793 out of revolutionary enthusiasm.

since it refers a man; nor does it concern Mulot or his wife, since they had no children[9].

The fifth and final piece of evidence shows that the annotators, whoever they may have been, were inexcusably careless. The first piece listed among the seized documents is a fifty-nine-page handwritten notebook entitled *Mon Apologie* (*My Apology*). Regnard, the secretary of the revolutionary Committee of Compiègne, signed and initialed each page. At the top of the first page one reads: *Par Mullot (sic)*. Therefore, did Mulot sign this document? No. Had he written or copied it? Not at all. Could he, in any capacity, be considered the author? It suffices to read the first lines in order to be convinced of the contrary: "I did not take the civic oath required by the decree of November. Out of honor and religion, I am accountable for my conduct to all my confreres in the priesthood." From these three opening lines, it was easy to recognize that this was a priest who had refused to take the schismatic oath and who believed he had to explain himself. However, Mulot de la Ménardière was notoriously a lay person, and married.[10]

In summary, for what could one reproach Mulot? A single line: that will be enough to ruin him.

---

9 Regarding this letter, Alexandre Sorel accused the Carmel of being frivolous in their remarks. He had neglected to read the letter to the end.

10 The author of this eloquent *factum*, which had its day of glory and against which Abbé Grégoire launched a polemic that the same author supported with a second pamphlet that had seven editions, was Monsieur François, a Lazarist Father, the superior in Paris of the Saint-Firmin or Bons-Enfants Seminary, located at the corner of *Rue des Fossés-Saint-Victor* and *Rue du Cardinal Lemoine*. It was because of this writing and his refusal to take the schismatic oath, before its publication, that, along with so many other victims, on September 3, 1792 Mr. François was massacred in the very seminary of which he was superior and which he had refused to abandon. *Mon apologie. (My Apology.)* s.l.n.d. in-8°, 40 p. *Défense de mon apologie contre M. Henri Grégoire* (*Defense of my apology against Mr. Henri Grégoire*). Paris. Crapart, 1791, in-8°, 48 p., seven editions. Bibl. nat., Ld, 3405 and 3443. In 1788, Monsieur François delivered and published a funeral oration for Madame Louise de France.

CHAPTER X

Imprisonment at the Visitation

(June 22 - July 12 – 4-24 Messidor Year II)

The Carmelites and Mulot were arrested and imprisoned on June 22–4 Messidor. Three days later, the revolutionary Committee of Compiègne sent the following letter to the Committee of Public Safety and General Security of the National Convention, which we transcribe *verbatim*:

> Equality, Liberty.
>
> On this 7th day of Messidor in the second year of the French Republic, one and indivisible.
>
> The Supervisory and Revolutionary Committee of Compiègne,
>
> To the representatives of the people comprising the Committee of Public Safety and General Security of the National Convention.
>
> Citizen representatives,
>
> Always on the hunt for traitors, our eyes are constantly on those perfidious individuals who dare to plot against the Republic, or who wish for the destruction of liberty. For a long time, we suspected the former Carmelite Nuns of this commune, although lodged in different houses, of still living in community, subject to the rules of their former convent. Our suspicions were not in vain; after several thorough searches having been made of their homes, we found correspondence of the most criminal nature. Not only did they hinder the progress of public opinion by welcoming into their homes persons they admitted into a Confraternity known as that of the Scapular, but they also made vows for counterrevolution, the destruction of the Republic, and the restoration of tyranny. You can judge for yourselves from the thirty-one documents we enclose herewith.
>
> After reading these documents, we did not hesitate to arrest these former Nuns.
>
> Here are their names:

Marie-Claudine Lidoine.

Anne-Marie-Madeleine Thouret.

Marie-Claude-Cyprienne Brard.

Marie Dufour.

Thérèse Soiron.

***

Marie-Gabriel Trézel.

Marie-Françoise Croizy.

Anne Pellerasse.

Angélique Roussel.

Elisabeth-Julie Vérolot.

Marie-Geneviève Meunier.

***

Marie-Anne Bridoux.

Rose Chrétien.

Marie-Anne Hanisset.

Marie-Anne Piécourt. [sic]

Catherine Soiron[1].

We note that the aforementioned Lidoine had a portrait of the tyrant in her pocket and had just brought back a relic from Paris with a certificate of authenticity.

This correspondence having identified the aforementioned Mulot, known as Laménardière, by means of a letter and a poem written in his own hand, we have also had him arrested as their accomplice.

As the crimes of which these individuals are accused fall within the number of those which the jurisdiction belongs to the Revolutionary Tribunal, we await your authorization, in

1 The reader will have made the corrections himself: Croissy, Pelras, Brideau. I would be inclined to believe that this order of names reveals the composition of each group at the time of arrest in the three houses.

accordance with Article II of the law of the 22 Prairial last, for their transfer to Paris; but if there is another course of action to be taken, please give us your orders in this regard.

Count on our zeal and vigilance, fellow citizens and representatives; we will always be able to unmask the scoundrels, whatever guise they may take.

Salutations and fraternity.

Signed: ROGÉE, DUCREY, LECLERC, BAILLET, BOURGEOIS, VALANSART ET TRÉZEL.

Counter-signed:

REGNARD, Secretary. DESMAREST, Ex-president.

***

The Carmelites ignored this denunciation, which mainly incriminated them of persisting to live in community, even though they were lodged separately. But, given the harsh treatment that they were subjected to, they could sense the fate that awaited them. They had to prove themselves worthy of it. However, since her trip to Paris, the Mother Prioress had been troubled by scruples regarding the legitimacy of the oath of liberty and equality that she and her Sisters had taken before the mayor on September 19, 1792. She knew that Bp. de Bourdeilles, the Bishop of Soissons, condemned it; and, that before the Revolutionary Tribunal in Paris, the Carmelites of the *Rue de Grenelle* had stubbornly refused to take it and had been sentenced to imprisonment for this reason. Were not the twenty-two months of relative tranquility they had enjoyed in Compiègne the price of a compromise? Isolated from all counsel, with no hope of communication either with her superior or with any priest she trusted, the more that the Mother Prioress understood that her destiny and that of her Sisters was leading them towards the sacrifice she had already made in her heart, and for which she had inspired the desire in her companions, the more she had to hope that even the appearance of an infidelity would not alter its merit. A decision had to be made, and, given the urgency of the circumstances, it had to be made quickly.

When, nine months later, Sister Marie of the Incarnation appeared before the municipality to hand out – her also – her oath, the mayor told her what had happened: "Your ladies had us summoned to the jail in order to retract their oaths. I tried in vain to dissuade them from this plan. All of them declared to us, with an unyielding determination, that they would rather die than take the oath. You will see for yourself from their signatures, which will be shown to you in the register," and, turning to the clerk, he added, "Citizen, show Madame..." She was indeed shown the retraction of her companions, "whose signatures," she said, "I kissed with respect."[2]

On what date did this retraction take place? As the denunciation of June 25 (7 Messidor) makes no mention of it, it must be concluded that this retraction took place after the denunciation: how could one suppose that anyone would have dared to omit such an aggravating circumstance from the accusation and conceal it from the Committee of Public Safety? It must therefore be dated not to the first days of their imprisonment, but to the end of June or to the first days of July. However, it would be possible that, in a private letter, some eager member of the Revolutionary Committee of Compiègne communicated this information either to the Committees of Paris, to the public prosecutor, or to the president of the Revolutionary Tribunal, Toussaint Scellier, the brother of the mayor of Compiègne.

---

2 This register has disappeared, and despite extensive research, Sorel has been unable to find it. Being that so many other documents relating to the revolutionary period have been removed by those involved who wanted to shelter themselves from reprisals or preserve their memory, it is not surprising that this one has suffered the same fate. The detailed testimony of Sister Marie the Incarnation must suffice. It should be noted, however, that the mayor who spoke to her in 1795 could not, given the political developments that had taken place, have been the same one who had received the retraction in 1794; but this is a secondary point.

The denunciation, the text of which we have given above, did not take long to produce its effect. On July 12–24 Messidor, the following decree arrived from Paris from the Committee of Public Safety:

Liberty. Equality.

THE NATIONAL CONVENTION

COMMITTEE OF GENERAL SAFETY AND SURVEILLANCE OF THE NATIONAL CONVENTION

On the 22nd day of Messidor, Year II, of the French Republic, one and indivisible.

Given the letter from the Revolutionary Committee of Compiègne dated the 7th of this month, to which were attached three packages, one containing twenty items, among which is found an engraving depicting Capet, found at the home of a woman named Lidoine, an ex-Carmelite residing in Compiègne; the second package containing nine items found at the home of a woman named Brard; the third containing two items found at the home of a woman named de la Vallée, all ex-Carmelite Nuns currently in Compiègne;

Whereas it appears from the aforementioned exhibits that the above-named individuals engaged in correspondence intended to incite internal disputes contrary to the principles of the Revolution and favoring crimes of tyranny; whereas, according to the letter from the Revolutionary Committee of Compiègne, the following individuals: Marie-Madeleine Thouret, Marie Dufour, Thérèse Soiron, Marie-Gabriel Trézel, Marie-Françoise Croisy, Anne Pellerasse, Angélique Roussel, Elisabeth-Julie Vérolot, Marie-Geneviève Meunier, Marie-Anne Piécourt, Catherine Soiron, Marie-Anne Bridoux, Rose Chrétien, Marie Annisset, the man named Mulot, known as La Ménardière, and the man named Guillemette, are guilty or accused of complicity in the same crimes;

Decree that the above-named individuals be brought before the Revolutionary Tribunal to be tried in accordance with the law; that the above-mentioned exhibits be sent to the clerk of the Revolutionary Tribunal;

Command that the Revolutionary Committee of Compiègne

has the individuals named in this present decree be brought to the Conciergerie.

The Representatives of the People, members of the Committee of Public Safety.

Signed: AMAR, VADIER, JAGOT, ELIE LA COSTE, LOUIS (du Bas-Rhin).

***

Based on the division of the parcels of evidence made by the Revolutionary Committee of Compiègne, it appeared that no more than three people, including poor Mulot, were, according to the justice of the time, liable to be charged: 1st Madame Lidoine, from whom twenty items had been seized, including the portrait of "Capet;" 2nd Madame Brard, who had kept, in addition to letters of a purely spiritual direction, or from relatives concerning only family matters, a letter and verses from Mulot; 3rd Finally, Mulot himself. As for Madame de la Vallée, mistakenly described as a Carmelite, she was, as we know, only the owner of the premises where Mesdames Brideau, Hanisset, etc. lived on the *Rue de la Liberté*, or *Rue des Cordeliers*. The other Carmelites, being alien to this correspondence, were only affected as Nuns participating in the life, exercises of piety, and sentiments of their companions, living close to them under the same Rule and under the same discipline.

The Committee of Public Safety had examined all the documents so hastily that, upon encountering the name of a certain Sir Guillemette, to whom a letter dated August 1792 was addressed, and that of Madame de la Vallée, specified as the owner, it had, without further investigation, included both names in the prosecution. Moreover, there had been no preliminary investigation, no inquiry, no information gathering of any kind: all of that would be done at the hearing – or rather, it would not be done at all.

This decree of 22 Messidor (July 10) must have reached Compiègne on the evening of July 23 or the morning of 24 Messidor (July 11 or 12). On the morning of 24 Messidor (July

12), the Committee of Surveillance met under the presidency of Ducrey, whose turn it was for the fortnight, and they decided to immediately carry out the order they had just received.

Consequently, it issued a decree whereby a national gendarme, accompanied by ten dragoons, were to take the sixteen Nuns whose names he gave, and also Mulot de la Ménardière, making a total of seventeen "guilty" persons, to the Conciergerie, near the Revolutionary Tribunal of Paris. The gendarme would travel alone to Paris, deposit his prisoners at the Conciergerie, and obtain a receipt from the warden, which would be signed by the public prosecutor. The municipalities were required to provide new carriages and a sufficient escort, as well as accommodation for the journey. The escort taken from Compiègne would stop at Senlis.

The national gendarme also carried the attached letter for the public prosecutor.

> Liberty, equality, fraternity, or death.
>
> Compiègne, 34 Messidor, Year II of the French Republic, one and indivisible.
>
> The Revolutionary Supervisory Committee of Compiègne,
>
> To the public prosecutor at the Revolutionary Tribunal in Paris.
>
> Citizen,
>
> Pursuant to the decree of the Committee of Public Safety, a copy of which we are sending you herewith, we have just sent seventeen guilty individuals, named in the said decree, to the Conciergerie. We have just informed the Committee of Public Safety that the man named Guillemette and his wife named La Vallée are not among the prisoners we have sent, as the aforementioned Guillemette never lived in our commune and disappeared from our area in 1790 (old style), and the citizen La Vallée was not included by us among the guilty parties, since she is only mentioned in our report as the owner of a house inhabited by some of the ex-Carmelites. Please sign the discharge given to the gendarme by the warden of the

Conciergerie.

Greetings and fraternity.

Signed: Ex-president Mosnier, Valansart, Potier, Regnard, Trezel, Baillet, Desmarest [and two other illegible signatures].

***

Once these arrangements had been made, the members of the Revolutionary Committee, accompanied by the mayor, the deputy mayor, the District National Officer, and followed by four gendarmes and as many dragoons, immediately went to the Visitation. That morning the Carmelites, who after much pleading had finally obtained permission to bleach their own laundry, had all set to work, the oldest and the youngest alike. They had barely begun, with the laundry soaking in the tubs, when the members of the Revolutionary Committee arrived with their entourage. They had the doors opened and informed the Sisters of the order for their immediate transfer to Paris. Mother Henriette of Jesus pointed out that the laundry was wet and needed to be dried and put back in order; moreover, it was lunchtime, and they had barely begun to eat their soup. "Go! Go!" said the mayor (Scellier Jr.), "You don't need anything, neither you, nor your companions. Hurry down, because the carriages are waiting for you." Indeed, two carriages filled with a sufficient quantity of straw had been ordered from citizen Cressent, a carriage driver; they were supposed to be in the courtyard of the convent, that is to say, the prison, at precisely two o'clock.

Were there any material preparations to be made? The words of Scellier were all too telling: behold, the road to Calvary was finally opening up. Each one had their hands tied. Mulot de la Ménardière, their alleged accomplice, was brought from another part of the house, and the seventeen victims, divided between two carts, were paraded before a screaming mob of women, among whom they could recognize some poor women whom they had helped in every way in the past: these women clapped their hands and hurled insults at the Nuns, saying that it served them right to be destroyed because they were useless mouths to feed.

At three o'clock, the carts started rolling along, carrying the Carmelites and their companion to Paris, escorted by two gendarmes and nine dragoons commanded by a Sergeant. "The Carmelites," wrote an eyewitness, one of the Benedictines of Cambrai who were then imprisoned at the Visitation, "left the prison of Compiègne like saints: we saw them embrace each other before leaving, and they bid us affectionate adieus with waves of the hand and other signs of friendship."[3]

3 Excerpt from the manuscript of Dame Ann Teresa Partington. *Procès apostolique.* (Apostolic Trial), p. 637.

CHAPTER XI

At the Conciergerie

(July 13-17, 1794 – 25-29 Messidor Year II)

Eight leagues separate Compiègne from Senlis: the procession, moving slowly, did not arrive until eleven o'clock at night. There, the horses and escort were changed. It was a moment of respite for the Sisters who, their hands bound, had been forced into a cruel immobility. Although it was night, they set off again: at this time of year, the day breaks early. We can imagine that communal prayer and the recitation of some Office interrupted their solitary meditations from time to time. At one league per hour, the second leg, which was thirteen leagues long, must have taken just as many hours. They therefore did not arrive in Paris until around three or four in the afternoon. There was no need, as has been said, to go from prison to prison: according to the travel plan, the Conciergerie was the intended destination. Due to the speed and number of daily executions, it was certain that there would be vacancies there, even if they were only from the previous day, or, at this late hour of the afternoon, from that very day.

The carts, with their escort, entered into the *Cour du Mai* and lined up on the right near the prison counter. On the steps of the grand staircase stood some men and women, who were waiting for the arrival of the prisoners or for their departure for the scaffold, savagely curious, among whom were a few others who were animated by better sentiments. However uncomfortable the Nuns must have felt at being put on display in this way, and despite the embarrassment resulting from having their hands tied, they got off the carts without incident. Only one, Madame Thouret, in religion Sister [Charlotte] of the Resurrection, the eldest (she was about to turn seventy-nine) and infirm moreover, could not support herself with her hands or her cane. Her limbs were numb from prolonged immobility, and her Sisters, who had already come down, were unable to help her as their hands were tied. Thus, she did not know how to get off and waited. Impatient with these delays, the drivers climbed into the cart and, grabbing the poor old woman, threw her brutally onto the pavement. Some of those present could not help but cry out: "Ah! Wretched men! You have caused her to die! You have killed her! Miserable wretches!" Indeed, she was believed to be dead, so still was she. She was lifted up, her face covered in blood, but turning to those who had mistreated her, she said, "Believe me, I do not hold it against you. I thank you for not killing me, for I would have missed out on the happiness of the martyrdom I await."[1]

Under these sad conditions, the Carmelites and their companion, Mulot de la Ménardière, entered the Conciergerie, a sinister and mysterious prison that envelops in its darkness the victims imprisoned within its walls. Who can tell us about our Carmelites, their attitude, their feelings, or the effect that sixteen Nuns must have had when they appeared among these women of the world, these priests, these nobles, and these artisans with whom they were to share their fate? We consulted the few known publications on prisons, but there is no mention of Carmelites. Riouffe, who was in the Conciergerie at the time, does not seem to have recognized them: dressed as Nuns, they might have been noticed, but in their secular clothes, how could they be distinguished from all the other women, arrested at random and indistinguishable from one another as the common prey of the scaffold?

July 13 was a Sunday; but at that time, since the establishment of the revolutionary calendar, Sunday was no longer a day of rest: the Tribunal was in session. To dispatch the judgments faster, two hearings were held simultaneously, one in the Hall of Equality, the other in the Hall of Liberty. The public prosecutor, Fouquier-Tinville, moved from one to the other,

1 "I have this from an eyewitness, Mademoiselle Fouchet." (Sister Marie of the Incarnation, printed account, p. 80).

sometimes appearing in person, sometimes delegating this task to a deputy. Thanks to this duplication, the Tribunal judged (if it could be called judging) 50 to 60 defendants per day, that is to say, in a maximum of four or five hours of hearings in each hall. Thus, on that very day, Sunday, July 13, in one of the rooms, four women, sixteen men of all professions, and eight priests were sentenced to death; in the other, ten individuals and two women. From the first day of their arrival at the Conciergerie, the Carmelites could hear the news of these condemnations and observe the comings and goings of their fellow prisoners, some going up to the tribunal to be tried, others coming down and passing back through the prison to be taken to the place of execution.

The next day, Monday, July 14, the anniversary of the storming of the Bastille, was a public holiday: the Tribunal and the executioner were off duty. On Tuesday, the 15th, the revolutionary machine began to function again: in the Hall of Equality, eight death sentences; in the Hall of Liberty, twenty-two. On Wednesday, the 16th, in the former, seventeen; in the latter, nineteen. These defendants came from Cognac, Ain, the Ardennes, Confolens, Moselle, and Haute-Loire, sent to the Tribunal by the public prosecutors of the departments, on the orders of the Committee of Public Safety: priests were no less present than women. In summary, three hearings, albeit double hearings, on Sunday, Tuesday, and Wednesday, were sufficient to sentence to death and execute 106 people, including 76 men, 17 women, and 13 priests. This rapid and multiple succession of condemnations created an atmosphere of death for the prisoners of the Conciergerie, where they lived, it is said, with indifference and some with ease: they entered there to die, they knew it, and it was the opposite that would have deceived their expectations.

A few months earlier, six Carmelite Nuns from the convent on *Rue de Grenelle,* along with a Visitandine Nun, had spent three days (February 7-9, 1794) at the Conciergerie: "We were put to sleep on straw," one of them recounted, "two to a bed, in large rooms that resembled cellars by reason of in their humidity and darkness. We were covered with vermin, which was no small suffering...No sooner had we entered than we were sought out to go and receive our letters of accusation...A most unpleasant clerk escorted us back to our new dwelling. There were sixteen of us there, and, fortunately for us, our companions turned out to be very fair."[2] We can perhaps infer from these few lines that the Carmelites were gathered in this same room where, already sixteen in number, they were not mixed with other prisoners.

Among those detained at the Conciergerie for the past month or two was Denis Blot, a vinedresser from Orléans. A Christian and an aristocrat, that is to say, not particularly disposed in favor of the revolutionary ideas or practices, he was convicted of hiding a refractory priest named Porcher, curé of Faronville (Loiret), who was condemned to death and executed in Orléans, on the *Place du Martroi*, on 27 Floréal Year II (May 16, 1794). Arrested and imprisoned at the Minims convent, Blot was sent to the Revolutionary Tribunal after two months in captivity. At the Conciergerie, he had won the favor of the warden, Richard, who had authorized him to make himself available to the parliamentarians from Toulouse, who were detained at the same time as him. Numbering twenty-two, they had just been tried, convicted, and executed (July 6).[3] He enjoyed a certain amount of freedom inside the prison. It seems certain that he saw the Carmelites and that, "through the window," he was able to render them minor services.

The custom in certain monasteries of Carmel, but especially in that of Compiègne, was to commemorate a feast or anniversary with some piece of poetry. These austere houses know no sadness: neither a certain gaiety nor the free expression of character and natural qualities are forbidden there. The Mother Prioress, Mother Henriette of Jesus, did

2 Wallon, op. cit., v. II, pp. 573-574.

3 Wallon, op. cit., v. 1. IV, p. 395.

not refuse herself this more or less poetic distraction. Was it necessary, in this prison, to consume oneself in somber meditations, to constantly keep one's mind at bay from thoughts, even appropriate ones, provoked by a future so close and so certain? Instead of strengthening oneself in this sole contemplation, one's moral energies could be broken or, at the very least, exhausted. As we know, the valiant Prioress, enamored and almost obsessed with this idea of martyrdom, it was up to her to support her companions in this final journey: no longer with the exhortations she had so often lavished on them, but with a cry of enthusiasm in which all of them would unanimously express their resolve, their confidence, and their **prayers.**

The Mother Prioress, perhaps with the help of one of her Sisters, had the idea of composing a few heroic verses to the tune of *La Marseillaise*, which would serve as a battle song. In verses improvised at such a time, one would not expect to find poetic and literary merit beyond that provided by *La Marseillaise* itself, but two things can be found there: first, the impulse of these souls toward their eternal destiny that was approaching; and second, the testimony of the feelings that sustained them in those moments of anguish.

The first verse recalls the song of Rouget de l'Isle: it is a cry of joy, a song of victory, a burst of zeal:

Let us surrender our hearts to joy!

The day of glory has arrived.

Far from us is the slightest weakness;

The bloody sword (repeat) *is raised.*

Let us prepare for victory

Under the banners of a dying God.

Let each one march as a conqueror!

Let us all run, let us fly to glory,

Let us rekindle our ardor,

Our bodies belong to the Lord.

Let us ascend, let us ascend
To the scaffold, and God will be victorious.

The third verse (we omit the second, which seems unfinished) confesses the fears and weaknesses of nature, but that from God that strength will come:

Great God, who sees my weakness,
I desire and I fear always:
Confidently, ardor urges me on;
But give me Your help (repeat).
I cannot hide my fear from You,
Thinking of prisons, of death.
Be, You alone, my comfort.
I say, No, no more constraint.

The last two verses are addressed to the Blessed Virgin: is she not the Queen of Martyrs? It is up to her to support her children, to present them to her Son.

Holy Virgin, our model,
August Queen of Martyrs,
Deign to support our zeal
By purifying our desires (repeat).
Protect France once again,
Watch over us from the heights of Heaven;
Let us feel in these places
The effects of your power, etc.

See, O divine Mary,
The holy transport of your children.
If we receive our lives from God,
For Him we accept death (repeat).
Show yourself to be our tender mother,

Present us to Jesus Christ,
And may we, animated by His Spirit,
When we leave this earth
For the heavenly abode
With the fire of holy love
Sing with the Saints His goodness forever!

***

One of the Sisters asked Blot, in the absence of pen and ink, for a few pieces of charcoal or burnt wood to write down this hymn: "I attest," said Sister Marie of the Incarnation, "to having transcribed this hymn from the original, written with burnt charcoal, which I believed to be the handwriting of my Sister Julie (Rose Chrétien). I tried in vain to solicit it from the pious young lady who had it in her hands and told me she had obtained it from a person confined in the Conciergerie who had been released, and who assured her that the said hymn had been written by the Carmelites: all my efforts to obtain the original were in vain, as the young lady regarded this piece, which can be seen as a parody of *La Marseillaise*, as a true relic."

This day of July 16th was a great feast day for the Carmelites: Our Lady of Mount Carmel. They celebrated it, as Blot observed; but in what manner? One can imagine: like prisoners, and how different from former times! No more friendly priest, like Abbé Bida, to deliver a sermon, to offer the comfort of his ministry, consoling exhortations, or the supreme gift of a final Holy Communion. A sad feast, if one considers only earthly feelings; but, a glorious vigil of a greater feast, for those who awaited martyrdom.

Vigil, I said. Indeed, on the evening of that day spent in contemplation of God, they received notice that the next day, July 17, they would appear before the Revolutionary Tribunal. Were they given a copy of the indictment? It is impossible to say. All these documents were being drawn up at the last minute; there were not enough clerks to do the work. It is quite possible that this document, dated 28 Messidor, that is to say, the day before the trial, was not delivered, and that a verbal notice was sufficient. This was, moreover, we are assured, the usual practice, and it was not uncommon for prisoners to be awakened early in the night, either to serve them with their indictment or to inform them in-person of their appearance in court the following day.

CHAPTER XII

The Hearing of the Revolutionary Tribunal

(July 17, 1794 – 29 Messidor Year II)

The law of 22 Prairial—June 10, 1794, which regulated or rather abolished all proceedings before the Revolutionary Tribunal, not only had the effect of depriving the defendants of any guarantees of defense; it also deprived history of these judicial investigations, which are one of its most valuable sources of information. When, a few months earlier (February 9), the Carmelites of *Rue de Grenelle* appeared before the Revolutionary Tribunal, which was then governed by the law of March 10, 1793, despite a few obstacles the defense had to overcome in order to reveal the truth, there was at least the recourse of the cross-examinations, either before the hearing by the president, or in public and at the hearing itself, which allowed the defendants to know the crimes of which they were accused and to respond to them. In this way, either through the account of one of these Nuns or through the notes of the clerk, we are able to follow the questions and answers, and one of the two documents serve to verify the other.

With the new law, there are no longer any specific and distinct crimes; they all boil down to a single one, that of conspiracy. Individual interrogation has been abolished; the minutes of the hearing, printed in advance, do not record anything that actually happened there. Witnesses are rarely summoned, as the court is free to dispense with them. There is no longer any defense. Since there is only one crime, that of conspiracy, and only one punishment, that of death, accusing and judging are one and the same thing, and just as the judge need make no effort to convict, the accused would make only futile efforts to escape the charge. Is the file opened? It is empty; the court records are silent; the judgment is modeled on the indictment; the same charge of homicide applies to all, and only the handwritten names (and even then, they are not always there) bear witness to the identity of the individuals who appeared before the Tribunal.

To supplement these judicial documents that hinder his research, the historian turns to the newspapers of the time, but his disappointment is no less complete. The Revolutionary Tribunal of Paris had a *Bulletin*; but the printer, who did not have the mechanical resources available today, could not keep up with the Tribunal. He fell several months behind and gave up trying to catch up. The Terror intimidated journalists: from February 1794 onwards, Prudhomme, the editor of *Révolutions de Paris* (*The Revolutions of Paris*), gave up and suspended publication. *Le Moniteur*, the *Journal de la Montagne*, and the *Thermomètre du Jour*[1] regularly and uniformly published the list of those condemned four or five days after the sentences were pronounced. *Le Journal des débats et décrets* (*The Journal of Debates and Decrees*) published nothing.

No pamphleteer, and no journalist dared to give the slightest detail about the hearings, the defendants, the judges, or the various circumstances of the judgments: all news, all opinion, and even all references to these things were stifled by a general rule of silence: the Convention respected it, and the Jacobin Club would not violate it. The work of the Tribunal was betrayed only by its results: every day, a few carts dragged the victims to the scaffold. Who were these victims? In a few days, their names would be known from the public newspapers; until then, they remained anonymous. As for the courtroom of the Revolutionary Tribunal, it was as if it had been pneumatically sealed, and let out neither noise nor echoes. For all these reasons, rather than making assertions, one had to often resign themselves to doubting or reserving judgment.

The hearing at which the Carmelites were to appear was held in the Hall of Liberty; it was the former Grand Chamber of Parliament, where Marie-Antoinette, the Girondins, Madame

1 [TN] *The Monitor*, *The Mountain Journal*, and *The Thermometer of the Day*

Roland, Danton, and so many others had been tried.[2] Two internal staircases connected it to the Conciergerie. It was via these narrow, slippery steps that the accused arrived and, once the verdict had been handed down, descended back into the prison.

Although we cannot retrace the feelings and state of mind that the Carmelites of Compiègne had on that morning of their final battle from their own accounts, is it daring to try to do so by evoking the testimony of those other Mothers of Carmel who, five months earlier, had faced the same ordeal? They too expected to die; they had prepared themselves for it with that courage and abandonment to the Divine Will which is characteristic of souls of this temperament, eager to suffer for God. "Sunday finally arrived," recounted Mother Angélique Vitasse, one of these Nuns. "We were so convinced that it would be the last day of our lives that we had all made our preparations for death. We were called to go up to the Tribunal: a universal trembling seized me. The warden took everything we had in our pockets, and a dozen men led us along many small dark pathways, very narrow, and very dirty; there were others that were very large and very wide. We climbed a great deal...The taunts we endured along the way from a large number of people who were waiting for us to pass were particularly painful for me to hear. I united myself as much as possible with Jesus, humiliated in His Passion, for love of me. We entered the hall amidst the noise of the whole crowd; but at that moment, a deep peace and calm came over me: I was so focused on God that I saw without seeing and heard without hearing. My Sisters had received the same grace and strength...What we felt was not the effect of a fevered mind, but the calm and peace that one experiences in Heaven. *Peaceful in the arms of our God, we wanted only to be faithful to Him, and we abandoned the rest to Him.*" Are these

2 After the Revolution, it became the civil chamber of the Court of Cassation; set on fire during the Commune of 1871, this site is now occupied by the first chamber of the civil Court of First Instance.

not the genuine feelings we can assume our Carmelites had at such a time, and would it be possible to portray them better?

The president of this section of the Revolutionary Tribunal was Toussaint-Gabriel Scellier, born in Compiègne on August 28, 1755, in the parish of Saint-Jacques. His father, a cloth merchant and captain commanding the Grenadier Company of the National Guard, died on October 25, 1790, leaving two sons: one, Alexandre-Pierre-Gabriel, whom we have mentioned several times as mayor of Compiègne; the other, the one we are now discussing. A lawyer in the bailiwick of Noyon, he had been appointed judge at the tribunal of Compiègne. This was a modest stage for his ambition and revolutionary ardor. In August 1792, he was called to Paris as commissioner of the Extraordinary Tribunal of August 17, from which he became a judge at the tribunal of the second arrondissement. On August 5, 1793, the Convention appointed him judge at the Revolutionary Tribunal: in this capacity, on October 14, 1793, he signed Marie Antoinette's death warrant at the Conciergerie, but he did not sit among her judges.

His harshness, his contempt for judicial procedures, his insolence towards the accused, and his rudeness were notorious and had recommended him, after the Law of Prairial, for the position of vice-president. He proved himself worthy of this choice; jealous of his colleague Dumas, he claimed to rival him in the swiftness of his summary judgments.[3] It was thus that in a single hearing, he dispatched the parliamentarians of Toulouse; that, in a few hours, he succeeded in condemning 51 defendants; that he led the prison conspiracies (Carmes, Saint-Lazare, Luxembourg) with great fanfare. Being from Compiègne, in other times, it would have been appropriate for Scellier to disqualify himself from judging his fellow citizens, but under the regime of perilous suspicion in which they lived, he had to show himself to be inflexible so as not to be accused of weakness.

3 [TN] A judgment without a hearing.

Sitting on the bleachers with their companion, Mulot de la Ménardière, the Carmelites formed half of a group of thirty-four accused individuals coming from various places, whom they did not know and could not know, brought from the Meuse and the Rhône, the Bouches-du-Rhône and the Bas-Rhin, the Ardèche and the Charente, from Paris also and its suburbs; people from all walks of life: shoemaker, musician, priest, wigmaker, mail carrier, cashier, businessman, clerk. One was an "officer of Brunswick;" another had made remarks about the Convention; another was insane. A fourth had lamented the fate of the *émigrés* and the orthodox priests who were being persecuted; this one had asked if his donkey was not in the commune council; that one had made other remarks. All of them, the Carmelites as well as the others, were accused of "having made themselves the enemies of the people and having conspired against its sovereignty." This diversity of people and crimes brought together under a single accusation had a name: it was called *amalgamation*.

The tribunal being assembled, after the customary address to the jurors, each defendant was asked their name, age, and occupation. The clerk then read the indictment, which was common to all the defendants but contained specific sections for each one. We need only consider here those concerning Mulot de la Ménardière and the Carmelites.

Our readers who know Mulot as a layman, married, and with his wife imprisoned in Chantilly, will be surprised that he could be described as a "refractory ex-priest." They will be no less surprised that this light-hearted man, a clumsy rhymester and indifferent Christian, was made the "leader of a counter-revolutionary gathering, a kind of Vendée hotbed, composed of Carmelite Nuns and other enemies of the Revolution."[4] How did this strange transformation take place? Common sense refuses to believe that it could have come from Compiègne: it must have originated in the offices of Fouquier-

4 This quotation and those that follow are taken verbatim from the extracts of the indictment.

Tinville. Seeing this middle-aged man (he was 53) in contact with Nuns and accompanying them, one concluded, without further reflection, that he was a priest and their chaplain. The manuscript, *Mon apologie*, with the heading "*Par Mulot*" ("By Mulot") confirmed this assumption.

The indictment went all out on this false trail: Mulot, considered a priest, is necessarily a counter-revolutionary, a deceiver, a hypocrite, an oppressor of consciences: "His correspondence with these women, who were subject to his will, reveals the counter-revolutionary principles and sentiments that animated him, and we note, above all, the profound deceitfulness familiar to these hypocrites, accustomed to presenting their passions as a manifestation of the will of Heaven." Everything was accepted into the body of evidence against them: the note addressed to his cousin, Madame Brard, inviting her to lunch with the Superior and another Sister; another note that is not in his handwriting and that only could have come from a priest: "You will join in the general intentions for the needs of the Church, etc.;" another note he received from his sister, in which the volunteers are described as lazy and devoid of manners; and finally, the four lines of verse that we know: "*The cold will destroy the insects,* etc." This was the only part of the accusation that had any foundation, and how miserable it was![5]

The main complaint against the Carmelites was their persistence in living according to their Rule: "Although separated by their residences, they nevertheless formed counter-revolutionary gatherings and secret meetings among themselves and others whom they assembled together."

These visits they made to each other, along with those persons they received for reasons of piety, were considered political acts. "By reviving this spirit of solidarity, they conspired against the Republic; a voluminous correspondence found in their homes shows that they never ceased to plot

5 *Supra*, "Seized Documents."

against the Revolution; the portrait of Capet, his will, the Hearts, rallying symbols of the Vendée, fanatical childishness accompanied by the certificate of a foreign or *émigré* priest, dated 1793,[6] prove that they were in correspondence with the external enemies of France. Such were the marks of the league formed between them; they lived under the obedience of a superior, and, with respect to principles and their vows, their letters and writings bear witness to these." We have quoted above the incriminating passages from these letters: our readers have been able to see whether they refer to politics and, above all, to a counter-revolution. There is no trace of correspondence with foreigners or *émigrés*. This letter from March 1793, to which allusion was made, was written by a young Nun, Victoire Pilloy, who spent so little time abroad that, on the very eve of writing her letter, she had met and (as she says) had chatted with the Carmelite Nuns in Compiègne itself. Residing in separate lodgings, as they had been ordered to do, were they forbidden to see each other, to visit each other as ordinary citizens? Or was it necessary, outside of the cloister, that they remain so confined to their homes so that each of their houses would become an even more enclosed cloister, and more secretive than their previous one?

This was followed by a few verses from the hymn to the Sacred Heart, and they claimed to pretend that "this counter-revolutionary hymn was, without a doubt, the one with which the priests of the Vendée led the blind victims of their wickedness to the murders and assassinations of their brothers." The young Victoire Pilloy, referring to the lifting of the siege of Maastricht, expressed the wish to be able to serve God more freely and to make reparation in a cloister (she had had to leave hers) for all her infidelities. "Thus," continues the indictment, "according to this conspiracy, it was necessary to shed the blood of men in order to restore the convents!"

A final allegation was that they refused to take the oath. Was their retraction known, which, in the jurisprudence of the

6 This certificate is not found in the dossier of the tribunal.

time, was equivalent to a refusal, or was this refusal inferred from those documents that revealed sentiments contrary to the oath of 1790? But on this point, there is no need to defend them: it was, out of all of the allegations, the only serious and well-founded one, and their conscience accepted it with joy.

The end of the indictment was nothing more than a furious tirade. It is necessary to quote it here in order to show the ridiculous tone in which these revolutionary-style documents were written: "They are nothing but a gathering, an assembly of rebels, of seditious women who harbor in their hearts the criminal desire and hope of seeing the French people return to the shackles of their tyrants and to the slavery of bloodthirsty priests, who are just as much impostors, and of seeing liberty engulfed in waves of blood which their infamous machinations have caused to be shed in the name of heaven."

Once this reading was complete, eight witnesses were heard: three for the defendants Debonne and Dupont, who would be acquitted; five for a certain Mr. Calmer, who would nonetheless be sentenced to death. For the Carmelites, as for Mulot de la Ménardière, no witnesses were heard, pursuant to Article 13 of the law of 22 Prairial: "If there exists material or moral evidence, independent of testimonial evidence, no witnesses shall be heard." Now, the material evidence was deemed to consist of the correspondence and documents in the dossier. As for the moral evidence, was there any other than the denunciations of "fanaticism" that weighed heavily on the indictment?

What happened then? Alexandre Sorel does not dare to say: he states that "the interrogation was very brief;" that the president "confined himself to making the Carmelites confess that they were nuns at heart;" that, moreover, the limited time available to the Tribunal, as well as its usual procedures, did not permit "any further discussion." However, he alludes to the interrogation found in the writings of Sister Marie of the Incarnation: "We cannot," he says, "either affirm nor deny this with absolute certainty, since no record of the proceedings, based on the testimony of anyone who was present, has come down to us. Moreover," he goes on to say, "Scellier was not ignorant that the Tribunal had thirty-four defendants to judge that day and would certainly not have allowed each of them to speak for so long." Mr. Wallon (*Histoire du Tribunal révolutionnaire de Paris,*[7] v. V, p. 52) is even more reserved, and although he draws inspiration from the book of Sorel everywhere else, here he abandons it. After having led the Carmelites to the foot of the Tribunal, he avoids recounting the hearing and even the execution. He was no doubt hesitant to venture into territory that he did not consider sufficiently historical and preferred to abstain.

Should we imitate this reserve and silence? Monsieur Jauffret, Abbé Guillon, Sister Marie of the Incarnation (their source of inspiration), without having been eyewitnesses, have passed on to us some accounts that they must not have taken lightly. Shall we reject these without examination, for the sole reason that there was no court reporter and that the official minutes are silent? Silent, as was customary; but even if there had been minutes, how could we trust them? They were printed in advance! Let us therefore see what Monsieur Jauffret and Sister Marie of the Incarnation have to say: their accounts form part of the record, and, while reserving the right to make certain observations that we feel are warranted, we should not deprive our readers of them.

Here is the text written by Sister Marie of the Incarnation, which is incidentally almost identical to the one written by Monsieur Jauffret. It is immediately apparent that she confuses Fouquier-Tinville, the public prosecutor, with President Scellier, and that she refers to the indictment as an act of denunciation: these confusions, on the part of a person ignorant of the terms of criminal procedure, are not surprising and are of no consequence.

"The President Fouquier-Tinville, holding the act of

7 [TN] *The History of the Revolutionary Tribunal of Paris.*

denunciation in his hand, said to them:

Q.– You are accused of having hidden weapons for the *émigrés* in your monastery.

The Mother Prioress, believing that the public prosecutor (the president) was addressing her more directly, immediately took a crucifix from her bosom and said to him: "Here, here, citizen, are the only weapons we have ever had in our house, and it cannot be proven that we have ever had any others."

Q. – You chose to expose the Blessed Sacrament under a canopy in the shape of a royal mantle.

A. – The canopy is an old decoration for our altar; its shape was in keeping with the decorations of this kind; there is no connection with the conspiracy with which they want to implicate us. I cannot believe that there is any seriousness in this charge.

"'But,' replied the President with an inconsistency calculated by malice and perfidy, 'this decoration indicates some attachment to the monarchy, and, by that very fact, to the deposed family.'"

"The Mother Prioress," observed Sister Marie of the Incarnation, "could have dispensed with explaining herself in response to a question that would have been ridiculous had it not contained a terrible trap; but, being no more capable of concealing her feelings for the Bourbon dynasty than of renouncing her God, she replied with all the boldness of a candid and sincere gratitude: 'If that is a crime, we are all guilty of it, and you will never be able to tear from our hearts our attachment to Louis XVI and his august family. Your laws cannot forbid this sentiment; they cannot extend their empire over the affections of the soul. God, God alone has the right to judge them.'"[8]

8 Monsieur Jauffret omits the part of this response relating to the royal family: this was undoubtedly out of fear of censorship. [EN: Jauffret wrote his book during the Napoleonic era. It was indeed not a good time for showing attachment to the Bourbon dynasty.]

Before moving on to the third charge, we must point out that none of these grievances are mentioned either in the denunciation by the Revolutionary Committee of Compiègne or in the indictment, which we have provided the reader with an accurate analysis of, including the main sections *verbatim*. Nor will the upcoming judgment make any mention of them. Under these circumstances, it does not seem that Fouquier-Tinville or Scellier had any reason to raise these questions. No document in the criminal dossier refers to these two charges, nor to the third, which we will examine shortly, nor does it make the slightest allusion to them. How could Fouquier-Tinville have known about this canopy? As for Scellier, it is understandable: he was from Compiègne. But would he, with his frenzy to move quickly, have asked these questions and tolerated such lengthy answers? I should not neglect to mention this point.

Let us move on to the third charge, again according to the text by Sister Marie of the Incarnation.

Q. – You maintained some correspondence with *émigrés* and sent them money.

A. – The letters we received were from the chaplain of our house, who was condemned by your laws to deportation;[9] the letters contain only spiritual advice. Furthermore, if this correspondence is a crime in your eyes, this crime concerns only me and cannot be the crime of the community, for whom the Rule forbids all correspondence, even with the closest relatives, without the permission of the Superior. So, if you need a victim, here I am: it is I alone whom you must strike, my Sisters are innocent.

The President. – They were your accomplices.

– If you judge them to be my accomplices, what can you accuse our two Externs of?

9 There are no letters from Abbé Courouble in the dossier, not even any from abroad.

The President. – Were they not your messengers, carrying the letters to the post office?

The Prioress. – But they were ignorant of the contents of the letters, and did not know where I was sending them, nor to whom I addressed them. Moreover, their condition as hired women obliged them to do as they were told.

The President. – Be quiet: their duty was to inform the nation."

"The scene is beautiful," someone said, "it would be unfortunate if it were not true." Although not scientific, the argument is nonetheless powerful. This scene, precisely because it is beautiful, should one believe it to be apocryphal? On the contrary, it is a reason why it cannot be the product of popular imagination. Besides, who would have invented it? We would not suspect Sister Marie of the Incarnation of whom "her truthfulness," says Monsieur Villecourt, "would not have allowed her to present as certain any fact that seemed doubtful to her" (Preface, p. 19). Will we attribute this honor to some eyewitness? The implausibility would be obvious. There is no doubt that Sister Marie of the Incarnation, as soon as prudence allowed her to leave her retreat, set out in quest of information about everything concerning her glorious companions. She could not have found any eyewitnesses to the hearing: her friends in Paris were not curious about such things; moreover, did they know, could they have known that the Carmelites had to appear in court? The only eyewitnesses were the Carmelites themselves, and I am inclined to think that it was one of them who, in the brief moments before departure for the place of execution, recounted the incidents to Blot, incidents so characteristic that they were engraved in his memory as easily as the features and names of the sixteen victims.[10]

---

10 Here is an example of the scrupulousness of Sister Marie of the Incarnation. Speaking of the death sentence, she writes: «This word of death....» Here, in the manuscript, we read: "me dit un témoin oculaire" (an eyewitness told me) but these five words are crossed out. In fact, Blot,

There is no need to dwell on the rest of the account of this Sister: "The Tribunal, considering itself sufficiently informed, Fouquier-Tinville, taking the floor, expressed himself in these terms." And the Sister reproduces verbatim the indictment that the clerk had read at the beginning of the hearing. Confusion reigns.

Let us move on to Mulot de la Ménardière.

Sister Marie of the Incarnation does not even mention his name. Monsieur Jauffret writes: "Mr. Mulot, accused of being their chaplain, underwent the same judgment. In vain did he protest against being labeled a refractory priest, which was said of him in the indictment; in vain did he attest to his judges that he was a husband and father;[11] that his wife was currently being held in the Chantilly prison; that he was not making any claims that could not be verified by the most authentic certificates; in vain did he invoke the testimony of one of his judges (Scellier), brother of the mayor of Compiègne, to certify the truth of his words: "I do not know you," replied the judge. However, we shall see that, while condemning him, his remarks were taken into account.

Did the Carmelites have a defender? Neither Sister Marie of the Incarnation nor Monsieur Jauffret mention one. It was not until 1835, in his note about the Carmelites of Compiègne[12] that Abbé Auger, curé of Saint-Antoine, wrote: "Mr. Sézille de Montarlet, of Noyon, had lent them the support of his talent and all the energy of his generous character." He belonged to a family from Noyon, whose leading members were imprisoned in Chantilly in August and September 1793. He

---

the person in question, did not attend the hearing and was not really an "eyewitness."

11 According to Sorel, the Mulot couple never had children.

12 *Notice sur les Carmélites de Compiègne* par M. l'abbé Auger. (*Note on the Carmelites of Compiègne* by Abbé Auger.) In-8° of 31 pages. Paris, 1835, Méguignon junior.

practiced as an unofficial defender[13] in Paris, a title given at that time to former lawyers, or those who usurped the name. In 1795, during the trial of Fouquier-Tinville, Scellier and their associates, Sézille de Montarlet appeared as the ninety-fifth witness, but he testified only on matters prior to the Law of Prairial.[14] The minutes of the hearing do not mention his name; he himself left no written or spoken record from which we can conclude that he was present in the Tribunal that day or that he spoke personally. He was not there, or he did not intervene. The question in itself is of little interest: before such judges, was a defense even possible? Moreover, Article 16 of the law of 22 Prairial stated: "For conspirators, the law does not grant defenders."

Thirty-four defendants sat on the benches. Four were acquitted. All the others were condemned to death for the same crime of conspiracy, but with varying circumstances.

Mulot de la Ménardière is no longer qualified as a "refractory priest" as in the indictment: this was the sole result of his defense. But for us, is this not proof that he defended himself and was heard? He was reputed to have conspired "by composing royalist and counter-revolutionary writings and by forming gatherings of fanatics at his home."

In the verdict of the Carmelites, there is no mention of the weapons they allegedly possessed, nor of the decoration/canopy resembling a royal mantle, nor of correspondence with *émigrés*, which would confirm our doubts about the reality of the three charges mentioned by Sister Marie of the Incarnation and Monsieur Jauffret. Unless the President did not desire to take the trouble to include them in the judgment, nor the clerk to transcribe them, contenting himself with the text of the indictment. They were convicted "for having formed counter-

13 [TN] *"défenseur officieux"* – a term used to designate the unofficial defense lawyers at the time of the Revolution (the office of lawyer having been abolished).

14 Bûchez and Roux, *Histoire parlementaire de la Révolution française* (The Parliamentary History of the French Revolution), v. XXXV, p. 73.

revolutionary gatherings and secret meetings, maintaining fanatical correspondence, and keeping anti-liberty writings as well as the rallying symbols of the rebels of the Vendée."

Here belongs a final scene that we find described by Monsieur Jauffret, Abbé Guillon, and Sister Marie of the Incarnation: "It is reported," she said, "that when our Mothers were summoned to the Tribunal, my Sister Henriette (Anne Pelras), having heard the public prosecutor call them 'fanatics' — a word whose meaning she knew well but which she pretended not to know — said to him, 'Would you kindly tell us, citizen, what you mean by this word *fanatic*?' The irritated judge responded only with a torrent of insults that he vomited at her and her companions. Our Sister, not at all disconcerted, said to him in a dignified and firm tone: 'Citizen, it is your duty to grant the request of a condemned person. I therefore summon you to answer and tell us what you mean by the word *fanatic*.' 'I mean,' said Fouquier-Tinville (or Scellier, the president), 'your attachment to childish beliefs, your foolish religious practices.' My Sister Henriette, after thanking him, turning towards the Mother Prioress said: 'My dear Mother and my Sisters, you have just heard the accuser declare to us that it is because of our attachment to our holy Religion...We all desired this admission: we have obtained it. Eternal thanks be given to the One Who first paved the way for us to Calvary! Oh! what happiness, what happiness to die for one's God.'"

Our readers will have noticed that Sister Marie of the Incarnation merely says, "It is reported," which suggests that she was somewhat reserved, at least about the details and the wording here. Monsieur Jauffret makes the story less dramatic and attributes it to all the Nuns and not to Anne Pelras alone. Here is his text, which seems to us to be closer to the truth and more plausible: "The judgment described the condemned women as *royalists* and *fanatics*. At this last word, these holy ladies could not help but betray their inner sentiments of their hope for immortality. For *fanatic* and *Christian* were then synonymous expressions, and to be described as such by their judges was to obtain written proof of a death suffered for the cause of the Faith."

Upon hearing the death sentence pronounced, one of the Externs, Thérèse Soiron, was overcome by sudden weakness and fainted. The Mother Prioress asked a gendarme to fetch a glass of water. But "this good girl," as Sister Marie of the Incarnation called her, quickly regained her senses and expressed her regret at having allowed herself to be caught in a moment of weakness.

CHAPTER XIII

The Sacrifice

(July 17, 1794 – 29 Messsidor Year II)

They had come descended from the Tribunal "with beaming faces," said Blot, an eyewitness. When he learned of their condemnation, he wept. "Why weep?" one of them said to him. "Are we not approaching the end of our troubles? Instead, pray to the good God and the Blessed Virgin that they may deign to assist us in these last moments. Tonight, we will be in Heaven, and on our part, we will pray for you." According to the same witness, it is reported that Madame Brideau, the Sub-Prioress, sold one of the mantles of the Nuns, and, with the proceeds, was able to buy each of her Sisters, who had been fasting since morning, a cup of chocolate. Following the shocks of the hearing, on the threshold of the terrible ordeal that remained to be faced, it was prudent to fortify the body for the final assault.

Their souls were ready. From early morning, their prayers, meditations, and thoughts had been fixed upon the event that was to end the day, the last one of their mortal lives, and the first of that one that would have no end. They had coveted martyrdom: the day had come. Courage would not fail them, but would nature not rebel, or weaken? This young Novice, barely twenty-eight years old; these two Sisters in their eighties, one of whom was infirm; these three Converse Sisters, whose faith elevated them to the point of sacrifice; these two Extern Sisters, above all, whom no threats, no fears had discouraged and who, without being bound by vows, remained inviolably attached to their Mothers: what would become of them, either on the way to the scaffold or on the scaffold itself? The Professed Mothers would endure the ordeal: but, could one, without presumption, hope for the same unshakeable resolve from the others? What a concern for the Mother Prioress, and how, burning herself with the thirst for martyrdom, she must have cast the same burning ardor upon the souls of her companions!

The preparations being complete, their hands bound behind their backs, as was customary, the Carmelites said their adieus[1] to those they had been able to see at the Conciergerie and passed through the doors.

In the *Cour du Mai*, several carts were stationed, between which the forty condemned prisoners of the day were divided (ten from the Hall of Equality, thirty from the Hall of Liberty). The sixteen Nuns were undoubtedly gathered on the same cart, under the watchful eye of the Prioress. It is not known whether Mulot de la Ménardière accompanied them or was separated from them[2].

1 [TN] "Adieu" in French implies a final, and forever goodbye. The literal meaning of the word comes combining «à» (to) and «Dieu» (God), literally meaning «to God» or «I commend you to God."

2 I believe I must dismiss the opinion according to which the Carmelites were clothed either in their white choir mantles, or even just in white. Blot, the last witness who had seen them leaving the Conciergerie; Blot, who had kept such a faithful memory of the name and appearance of each of them, says nothing about their attire. Sister Marie of the Incarnation, who wrote after him, maintains the same reserve. In a circular dated January 15, 1835, concerning the reestablishment of a monastery of Carmelites in Compiègne, the Reverend Mother Camille de Soyecourt makes no mention of this mantle and refers to the account of the martyrdom in a note in Delille's poem, *Malheur et Pitié* (Misfortune and Pity). Delille makes no mention of it either. A work, considered by the Carmelites to be based on documents of the most indisputable authenticity, printed in Reims in 1894 with the Imprimatur of Cardinal Langénieux, not for sale but distributed to the monasteries of Carmel, recounts (v. II, p. 268) the martyrdom of July 17, 1794, without any reference to the white mantle. The Reverend Mother Prioress of the Carmel on *Rue d'Enfer* has done us the honor of sending us the following lines on this subject: "I will venture to speak to you about a detail that only experience can appreciate. The opinion has recently been expressed that the martyrs were donning their white Carmelite mantles when they went to the scaffold. Certainly, if these mantles were at their disposal, they did not fail to wear them on their way to their death; but if one considers the weight and volume of one of our heavy woolen [lit. *bure*] mantles, it would be difficult to believe that the Carmelites, who had long lived in secular houses without the religious habit, could have taken their

It is a general tradition, found elsewhere other than in the writings about our Nuns, that as soon as they climbed into the carts, they began to sing or chant (the latter practice was more according to the custom in Carmel) the *Salve Regina* and the *Te Deum*. Someone thought that, given the time of day, they must have chanted the psalms of Compline, and then, at the end, the *Salve Regina*. It must be remembered that a double line of the National Guard kept the crowd at a distance from the procession, and that it would have been difficult for spectators to make out the nature of the songs, especially if they sang only in a low voice.[3]

Passing through the gates of the Palace, the procession went along, as usual, the *Rue Saint-Barthélemy,* named after the abandoned church of the same name. It was situated opposite the Palace, on the site now occupied by the Commercial Court. The procession would then cross over the *Pont au Change* bridge. From there, turning right, it followed the riverbanks and, taking the *Place Baudoyer,* near the Church of Saint-Gervais, entered onto the *Rue Saint-Antoine.* It was often on the steps of the Church of Saint-Louis that the priests stood, disguised in a *carmagnole,*[4] giving absolution to the

---

mantles with them when they went to prison. Had they even kept their religious habits at home? There is no trace of them in the inventories made by the municipality of Compiègne. A complete Carmelite habit, even when neatly folded, is bulky and could not be easily concealed." The reserve that history has a duty to maintain, on this point, does not concern painters. Their art consists of speaking to the eyes, so it is understandable that, when it comes to Carmelites, they depict them in the garb that allows the viewer to recognize them.

3 The custom of singing on the way to the scaffold was not so rare at the time. The Girondins did not have this privilege; but in Bordeaux, Cambrai, Orange, and later in Valenciennes, Nuns gave themselves this pious satisfaction without being prevented from doing so. *Illi quidem, ibant gaudentes... quoniam digni habiti sunt pro nomine Jesu contumeliam pati.* – "And they indeed went...rejoicing that they were accounted worthy to suffer reproach for the name of Jesus." (Acts 5:41)

4 [TN] A short jacket worn by working-class militant «*sans-culottes*» adopted from the Piedmontese peasant costume whose name derives from

victims. This practice, which involved some secrecy, was undoubtedly unknown to Sister Marie of the Incarnation: she makes no mention of it. Better informed, Monsieur Jauffret writes: "This kind of assistance was not lacking for the Nuns of Compiègne. All the priests who devoted themselves to this painful last duty had to fulfill it this time for their own consolation, and follow these holy victims with their blessings and good wishes." While not "all" of them were there, we are able to at least assume that, since Thursday was the day assigned to Abbé Renaud, it was this cleric who would have performed his pious duty for the Carmelites.[5]

They crossed the *Place de la Bastille*, still littered with the ruins of the fortress. The *Faubourg Saint-Antoine* then opened up, a wide road which led to the *Place du Trône*. Was the crowd furious and screaming, as Delille recounts, who could only speak from hearsay? Or, on the contrary, as Sister Marie of the Incarnation says based on other accounts, did they maintain a gloomy silence? It is likely that, over such a long distance, the mood of the crowd varied: here, violent words, shouts, and insults; there, groups animated by entirely different feelings. On the one hand, courtiers were summoned for the executions; elsewhere, there were local residents who did not want to miss the spectacle, though who were only interested out of curiosity. Among these rows of spectators, there were not only Jacobins from the revolutionary sections: how many souls must have been moved at the sight of this compact group of sixteen women who, recollected, praying, singing, and chanting, as they went forward to death with a heavenly demeanor and radiant faces! "Oh! those good souls," someone allegedly said; "I bet they will go straight to Heaven. Oh! yes, or else, there would be no Heaven." (Sister

---

the town of Carmagnola.

5 Abbé Renaud was a pseudonym (*un nom de guerre*): Monsieur Béchet, the delegate of Bishop de Juigné, had entrusted to seven priests the delicate ministry of assisting the condemned. It would be impossible to say which of the seven priests was bearing this name.

Marie of the Incarnation).

They arrived. The Carmelites descended from the cart and gathered around the Mother Prioress. At this terrible endpoint, they had the privilege that instead of being isolated and reduced to their personal courage, as their fellow prisoners, and as so many others had been, they would be able to die as they had lived: each supported by the energy and example of all, long prepared for this sacrifice that they had anticipated and desired. For these willing and seasoned victims, their execution would be mysteriously shrouded, if I may say so, in the ceremonies of a community exercise.

The supreme hour has struck. No adieus: what is the point when death will separate them only for a few moments? Together, with one heart, they renew their vows; together, they intone the *Veni Creator*; then the youngest, Constance Meunier, a Novice since 1789, kneels at the feet of the Prioress, gathering the words of blessing from her lips, and, as she would have done in the convent, asks her for one last permission: the permission to die. She then breaks away, climbs the stairs, and presents herself to the executioner. Thus, taking turns one by one, with the sound of the songs that continue to fade, the other Nuns do the same, until the Mother Prioress, like the mother of the Maccabees, climbs up last, assured of the fidelity of her daughters, whom death has joined back together.

It was noted that in the face of this religious and imposing spectacle, "the executioner, the guards, and the people showed no sign of anger or impatience." The drums fell silent and the usual spectators of these massacres forgot to applaud.

CHAPTER 14

THE BURIAL

Thus died, on the evening of July 17, 1794, the sixteen Carmelite Nuns of Compiègne.

A few hours later, all these mutilated remains were transported, along with those of the twenty-four others condemned that day, seven or eight hundred meters away and thrown haphazardly into a deep sand quarry that the municipality of Paris, by order of the recent 22 Prairial – June 10, had designated for the burial of those persons executed at the *Place du Trône*. Since June 14, nearly 1,200 had already been buried there: another hundred or so would be brought there until 9 Thermidor – July 27. In thirty-one days (since three days of the *décadi*,[1] when the court did not sit, must be deducted), there were 1,307 victims, or an average of forty-two per day.

This cemetery from the most violent period of the Reign of Terror still exists today.

A few days after the execution of the Prince of Salm-Kirbourg,[2] (5 Thermidor – July 23), his sister, Amélie-Zéphyrine of Salm-Kirbourg, Princess of Hohenzollern, bought the site of the mass grave with a few meters of land around it, which she enclosed. A little later, Mesdames de la Fayette and de Montaigu, daughters, sisters, and granddaughters of the three ladies of Noailles, who had perished on the same day (4 Thermidor – July 22, 1794), acquired a portion of land that had belonged to the canonesses of Saint-Augustin, which was adjacent to the pit, and built

1 [EN] The new revolutionary week, made of ten days.

2 A German prince, field marshal in France, head of the National Guard battalion (Grenelle fountain section), owner of the hotel located on *Rue de Lille*, which became the Palace of the *Légion d'honneur*. Involved in the so-called Carmes prison conspiracy, he was convicted along with 46 others. Wallon, *op. cit.*, v. V, pp. 81-95.

an oratory there. They established an annual memorial Mass, then a daily Mass. This initiative did not stop there: in the wake of a circular written by Lally-Tollendal, a subscription, which quickly rose to 40,000 francs, it was made possible to purchase the garden and enclose it with walls. The families of the victims obtained the authorization to have each of their own burial vaults there. Thus, side by side, separated only by a wall and an iron-barred gate, lie two cemeteries: one for the victims, the other for their families.

Around 1805, the care of this double cemetery was entrusted to the Sisters of the Sacred Hearts of Jesus and Mary, or of Picpus, founded during the Revolution itself by Madame Aymer de la Chevalerie. This final resting place of the victims of the Terror and so many illustrious deceased persons is well worth a pilgrimage. It is located at the end of the *Faubourg Saint-Antoine*, on *Rue de Picpus*. The house at No. 33 belonged to the Fathers of Picpus, whose chapel contained the remains of their brothers who were shot by the Commune in 1871; the law of July 1, 1901, drove them from their home and scattered them. The Nuns (at No. 35) still run a large school for young girls.

In the first courtyard stands a large chapel, surmounted by a dome. One enters. At the foot of the altar, in the presence of the Blessed Sacrament continuously exposed, two Nuns, wrapped in purple cloaks, kneel in a motionless attitude of contemplation that strikes one with admiration. On the walls of the sanctuary, two large white marble diptychs, divided into columns, lays bare the list of the 1,307 victims in the order of their executions. Every day in this chapel, a Mass is said for them and their families. Each year, on June 14 and July 27, that is to say, on the dates that marked the beginning and end of the period of the executions at the *Place du Trône*, a solemn memorial service is celebrated.[3]

3 The names of the sixteen Carmelites appear in the fourth column, on the Epistle side, from No. 924 to No. 939.

Upon leaving the chapel, passing through an orchard that serves as a promenade for the Nuns, one enters through a first enclosure: this is the family cemetery. The first tomb visitors encounter is that of Count Charles de Montalembert, the illustrious Catholic orator; on other tombs, we read the names of the Gouy d'Arcy, Quélen, Lasteyrie, Rémusat, and the Noailles Families; the Count of Mesnard, squire to the Duchess of Berry, and his daughter, the Marquise de Rosanbo; Abbé Le Rebours, curé of Sainte-Madeleine, grandson of a Parisian parliamentarian, who was one of the victims of June 14, namely, the first day of the executions at the *Place du Trône*, etc. At last, at the back on the right, the tomb of General Marquis de la Fayette, to which Americans from the United States, passing through Paris, never fail to make a pilgrimage of national gratitude.

Across a gate, a large square of lawn comes into view, planted with half dozen scraggy cypress trees: in the middle, an iron cross. The Family of Salm-Kirbourg, the owners of this mournful enclosure, have exercised their right of burial there, as attested by very modest stone monuments with inscriptions. The first, in front of the others, bears the name of Monsieur de Salm-Kirbourg, the victim of 1794, under which his mother has since been laid to rest, not far from her son;[4] two on the right and two on the left bear the dates 1827, 1840, 1859, and 1866: the last member of the family to be buried there did not want any stone or inscription to mark his grave.

This plot of land, almost bare, surrounded by walls, is the place where the victims of the *Place du Trône* were piled up. For 110 years, no excavation, even the most respectful, has disturbed their repose. Apart from those of the Salm Family, there are no monuments or tombstones.

4 "Here lies the body of Frédéric, reigning prince of Salm-Kyrbourg, sacrificed during the Reign of Terror on July 3, 1794, aged 49. His mother, who died in 1783, was exhumed and reunited with the object of her affection, upon this land that became the property of the family. — Pray to God for the repose of their souls."

To the left of the gate, inside the first cemetery, there is a marble plaque measuring 2 meters-high by 1 meter-wide: it was placed there on January 14, 1898, in the presence of two Fathers from Picpus and Bp. de Teil, the Vice-Postulator of the cause for the Carmelites, assisted by Monsieur Abbé Jacquet, an ecclesiastical notary.

It bears the following inscription:

IN MEMORY

OF THE 16 CARMELITES OF COMPIÈGNE

WHO DIED FOR THE FAITH

ON JULY 17, 1794

Madeleine-Claudine Lidoine, of Paris, Reverend Mother Thérèse of Saint-Augustine, Prioress.

Brideau, Sister Saint-Louis, of Belfort.

Piedcourt, Sister [Marie] of Jesus Crucified, of Paris.

Thouret, Sister [Charlotte] of the Resurrection, of Mouy (Oise)

Brard, Sister Sainte-Euphrasie, of Bourth (Eure).

De Croissy, Sister Marie-Henriette, of Paris.

Hanisset, Sister Thérèse of the Heart of Mary, of Reims.

Trézel, Sister Thérèse of Saint-Ignatius, of Compiègne.

Chrétien, Sister Julie, of Loreau (Eure-et-Loir).

Pelras, Sister Henriette, of Cajarc (Lot).

J. Meunier, Sister Constance, of Saint-Denis.

À. Roussel, of Fresne.

A. M. Dufour, of Beaune.

J. Verolot.

Catherine Soiron, Extern, of Compiègne.

Thérèse Soiron, Extern.

Their bodies repose behind this wall.
Beati mortui qui in Domino moriuntur.[5]

5 [TN] *"Blessed are the dead who die in the Lord."* (Ap. 14:13)

CHAPTER XV

At Compiègne

(1794-1795)

Four days after the Carmelites were sent to Paris, on the 28 Messidor (July 16), the eve of their appearance before the Revolutionary Tribunal, the mayor of Compiègne and two members of the district went to the Visitation prison and, stopping at the quarters of the English Benedictines, invited them, as they had already done several times before, to abandon their religious habit. In addition to their reluctance to comply, the Nuns had another major reason for refusing: they lacked the money to replace their worn-out garments. The mayor withdrew to the Revolutionary Committee and proposed, in order to resolve the difficulty, that the Benedictines be given, on loan, the garments that the Carmelites had been unable to take with them. The Committee, learning that these Benedictines were "still wearing wimples, guimpes, and habits whose gaudiness could only offend republican sensibilities," agreed to the mayor's request, considering that there could be "no better or more justified use for these items." They instructed two of their members, Valansart and Bourgeois, to deliver these clothes to the warden of the prison.

All that remained was to persuade the Nuns. The mayor returned to them and, taking two aside, told them that he could no longer tolerate the wearing of this "uniform," as he called it, which was prohibited by law: "If the people rioted," he said, "it would be easier for them to escape in civilian clothes." But as the Nuns repeated their objections, especially that of lack of money, he went into the neighboring room that had been occupied by the Carmelites; he brought back the various garments they had had to leave behind, still wet and "fresh from the tub," and gave them to the Benedictines with orders to put them on as soon as possible. In addition to thirty-four bonnets and thirty-four headscarves, there were seventeen sheath dresses or negligees, that is, as many as there were Carmelites, including Sister Marie of the Incarnation, whose return from Paris had been awaited; the Benedictines were equal in number.

"We were in great need of shoes," continues the Benedictine Nun who witnessed this scene, «so the mayor kindly told us that he would provide them also; but one of the jailers abruptly told the cellarer that we would not need them for long. As he left us, the mayor turned to Reverend Monsieur Higginson (their chaplain) and said to him: 'Take good care of your companions,' as if to say, 'Prepare them for death.' Indeed, he was powerless to do anything else, and the mayor knew it well. The next day, the news spread that the Carmelites had all been guillotined. The old garments, which only the day before had seemed so worthless, became so precious in our eyes, that from that moment on we considered ourselves unworthy to wear them. However, forced by necessity, we had no choice but to put them on."[1]

During the same meeting, the Committee, addressing the issue of the other effects belonging to the Carmelites and Mulot de la Ménardière that had remained in the prison, ordered that some be transported to *Rue de Dampierre* (*Saint-Antoine*), to the house where the Mother Prioress had lived, and others to the home of Mulot in *Faubourg de la Montagne* (*Saint-Germain*).

One can imagine the painful impression that the news of the execution of the Carmelites must have made on most of the population of Compiègne: but among those who were called the constituted authorities, the only effect that can be perceived was manifested in measures similar to the previous one.

Three days after the execution (the news had probably just been received), on Sunday, 2 Thermidor (July 20), the district council ordered the sale of some perishable food supplies,

1 Manuscript already cited by Dame Ann Teresa Partington.

such as honey, flour, and olive oil, which had been left at the residence on *Rue Saint-Antoine*. On 8 Thermidor (July 2) – which, as we know, was the day before Robespierre was overthrown and the staff of the Revolutionary Tribunal, Fouquier-Tinville, Herman, Dumas, and Toussaint Scellier of Compiègne, who had condemned the Carmelites, were arrested and thrown into prison –, the former mayor, Mr. de Cayrol, a judge at the Tribunal, was commissioned by the same Council to make a descriptive inventory of the furniture and effects that had belonged to the ex-Carmelites in the houses they had occupied. He was to be accompanied by two municipal officers, a member of the Revolutionary Committee, and the upholsterer, Lévêque, to assess the value of the items inventoried. This inventory lasted until 25 Thermidor (August 12), 1794.

The death sentence handed down by the Revolutionary Tribunal resulted in the confiscation of the property of those condemned for the benefit of the State. On 15 Thermidor (August 2), the national officer wrote to the members of the nine districts of the Oise department, to invite them, as a result of the death sentence handed down to the Carmelites and Mulot de la Ménardière, to immediately clarify the nature and extent of the property owned by each of the condemned persons, in order to proceed with their seizure, in accordance with the judgments.

On 21 Thermidor (August 8), lest anything be wasted, the pharmaccutical drugs found in the houses of the Nuns were given to the Philanthropic Society. On 9 Fructidor (August 26), Valansart, a notary, was charged with making an inventory of the furniture and effects that Mulot had left in his house in the *Faubourg de la Montagne*, subject to the rights of Madame Mulot, who was still being held in Chantilly, and Mulot's heirs, who had given Beaugrand, the former curé of Saint-Germain, the power of attorney to represent them. Finally, on 29 Vendémiaire Year III (October 20),[2] they proceeded with the sale of the furnishings of the Carmelites.

To avoid revisiting these repugnant details, let us skip forward a year.

On 11 Brumaire Year IV (November 2, 1795), the former monastery of the Carmelites, after serving as a temporary barracks and then as a field hospital under the name Jean-Jacques-Rousseau Hospital, was sold at auction: a man named Féret, a mason in Compiègne, won the bid for 950,000 livres payable in *assignats,*[2] which represented, at the rate of the time, 15,000 livres in cash.[3]

While all these procedures were being carried out, erasing little by little, at least physically, the traces of the Carmelites' stay, one of those whom a momentary absence, caused by pressing necessities had kept away from Compiègne and separated from her companions, Sister Marie of the Incarnation, returned to this city where so many poignant memories awaited her.

We left her in Paris on June 21, just as the Mother Prioress was leaving for Compiègne, expecting to see her again in a few days. As for her, following the permission she had received, she went to Gisors to spend the four or five days she needed to wait to finally obtain clearance from the authorities. When she returned to Paris, which must have been around June 26, she learned that, the day after her return to Compiègne, the Mother Prioress had been arrested, along with all her Sisters. What was she to do? Given circumstances that she could attribute it to the will of Providence, depriving her of the honor of "sharing," as she said, "the crown of her dear companions," was she to return to Compiègne to deliver herself into the hands of her persecutors? Would she remain in Paris, in "this place of abomination and horror," as the Mother Prioress had

2 [TN] The paper money issued by the French Revolutionary government (1789-1796) backed by confiscated Church and émigré lands.

3 I have borrowed this diverse information from the procedures related to the movable and immovable property of the Carmelites and Mulot de la Ménardière found in the documents published by Alex. Sorel, op. cit., pp. 73-76.

said, and where she risked being arrested in her turn? Neither of these options were acceptable to her, so she left Paris.

There is a certain obscurity surrounding this part of her life, as it did later over others. Here is what Monsieur Jauffret recounts: "Towards the end of June, she departed from Paris and had made plans to go to Switzerland. She even reached the frontier, but as the border crossings were not open, she made for Besançon. It was at an inn that she learned of the glorious end of her companions and heard some Christian travelers say: 'We must hope that our troubles will soon be over, for they have caused the death of several holy Nuns.'"[4]

As she made her way to Franche-Comté, did she not intend to seek temporary asylum with Madame Lidoine, the mother of the Prioress, who had undoubtedly just arrived in Ornans? We can only speculate.

In the note preceding the *Relation*, Monsieur Villecourt is hardly more explicit. He attributes to Sister Marie of the Incarnation a nomadic existence of one persecuted, the reasons for which are not entirely clear: "If the circumstances," he writes, "which Heaven had arranged, had spared her from death, it was only, in a way, to subject her to a longer martyrdom. Shall I recount what she had to endure, either in the mountains of Switzerland [so she went there?], where she was reduced for some time to eating grass in the fields, like animals, to appease the cruel hunger that devoured her, or in France, where she wandered from place to place, always sought after, always pursued?" Monsieur Villecourt suggests that this persecution was due to her lineage, "which, in the eyes of the law, was an even greater crime than her state as a Nun." Let us respect this mystery and continue: "The hardships of all kinds that she had endured, suffering from hunger, thirst, the rigors of the cold, the most excessive heat of summer, the snow and rain, the forced marches to which she had been subjected: all this had greatly altered her health,

4 M. Jauffret, op. cit., p. 373.

already naturally weak and delicate."[5]

At the end of March 1795, she arrived in Compiègne. The Committee of Public Safety and the Committee of Legislation had authorized that her belongings be returned to her in kind without being put up for sale, and had even taken it upon themselves to send the items to the authorities in Compiègne. The latter initially objected that the seals would only be lifted on the anniversary,[6] that is to say, in July. This was a strange objection; how could this anniversary affect her, since she had escaped conviction and her property was not subject to confiscation? But there was another reason: as we have seen, the furniture and effects of the Carmelites had been sold since October 27, 1794, and those belonging to Sister Marie of the Incarnation had been included in the sale.

Her concerns were of a higher order. Long deprived of any spiritual succor, and undoubtedly unable to find any in Compiègne, she went to Soissons, and, having found a way to enter the prison where the Vicars General, the depositaries of the powers of the Bishop, were being held, she begged one of them to hear her confession. We already know what the sentiments of Monsieur de Bourdeilles were regarding the oath of liberty and equality: Sister Marie of the Incarnation was well aware of them. The Vicar General first asked her if she had taken the oath: "I replied," she recounts, "that it had not been our intention, but that we have been deceived into signing it. A year ago, I added, I renounced my pension. 'That is not enough,' replied the vicar general. 'It is the retraction of it that we require. Wait, if you wish, until the storm has passed a little; but do not come before us until you have done so.'" One might be surprised at this severity. Sister Marie of the Incarnation would have found more indulgence among the delegates of the Archbishop of Paris, but the vicars general of Soissons had orders from their Bishop, and were they not

5 *Op. cit.*, preface, pp. 24-25.

6 [TN] i.e. July 16, 1795, the anniversary of the Carmelite Nuns being martyred.

themselves in prison for bearing witness to their beliefs and their doctrine? Moreover, Sister Marie of the Incarnation should have been all the less surprised, as she was of the same opinion.

She returned to Compiègne that evening and reported to "our little society of good Catholics" about a mission they had entrusted to her, but without telling them either what she had been told or what her intentions were. The next day, she left around ten o'clock to go to the Town Hall, but not without putting a diurnal and a nightcap in her pocket, "so as not to be caught unprepared in case I was taken to prison," she said. This precaution was characteristic of the era.

She entered the room where the mayor and municipal officials were gathered: everyone stood up. So they recognized her! This mark of courtesy surprised her. Was she unaware that, since January 14, the municipal council had been replaced, that Scellier Jr. had been replaced as mayor by de Vismes, and that, on March 23, the Revolutionary Committee, also replaced several months earlier, had just concluded its proceedings? Let us add that the law of 3 Ventose (February 21, 1795), had proclaimed the freedom of worship, except, it is true, to restrict it in an insulting manner and to keep it under the threat of multiple crimes and penalties. No matter! A breath of freedom had swept through the air, and the general spirit was no longer one of persecution.

Sister Marie of the Incarnation felt the solemnity of this encounter. "I say with the emotion of a deeply moved soul: Citizens, you must feel how much it must cost me to appear before the executioners of my community. Your city has been stained with three blemishes, three indelible crimes. It is the city that handed over the Maid of Orleans, the unfortunate Bertier,[7] and my virtuous and holy companions. I, whom

7 Bertier de Sauvigny, the son-in-law of Foulon, and intendant of the generality of Paris, was kidnapped on July 21, 1789, from his home in Compiègne on *Rue de la Porte-Paris,* and taken to Paris where he was massacred the next day.

Heaven did not judge worthy to be associated with their glorious death, was thus spared from the justice of men: I will not be spared from the justice of God. I come, therefore, before Heaven and earth to retract the aforementioned oath of liberty and equality, as contrary to the principles of our Mother, the Holy Catholic, Apostolic, and Roman Church. Consequently, I request that my retraction be recorded in your registry and that the document be delivered to me." Clearly, her declaration was proud, explicit, and bold; and had the vicar general of Soissons been able to witness it, he would have been greatly satisfied.

The mayor then explained to Sister Marie of the Incarnation how, despite his personal efforts, the Carmelites had retracted their oath. He showed her their signatures in the registry and invited the clerk to write down what she was about to say. The clerk was Thibaux, that former pastor of Saint-Antoine who, although juror, had shown consideration for the community at the time when Abbé Courouble said Mass for them at his parish. "I dictated to him word-for-word," she adds, "the formula of my retraction, and noticed, while he was writing, that his hand was trembling and that large tears were rolling down his cheeks. 'You must have great courage, Madame; I fear for you the consequences of a step that may be considered reckless.' — 'May the effort you have just made, Monsieur,' I said to him, 'procure you the same grace from Heaven!'" There is no document to suggest that Sister Marie of the Incarnation had suffered, either immediately or later, as a result of her bold declaration.

This act, which was dear to her heart, having been accomplished, Sister Marie of the Incarnation remained in Compiègne for some time. The final period the Carmelites spent outside of the cloister, brought them closer to the Catholic community of the city and allowed them to forge friendships that the persecution would not fail to strengthen. Since the month of May 1794, when she had left Compiègne, how many events had taken place in Compiègne itself! The last weeks of freedom that she had not shared with her Sisters; imprisonment at the Visitation, the harsh and painful life of the prison, departure for Paris: all of these events mixed with much bitterness, were they not also mixed with some sweetness while recounting them in conversations with friends, in gathering testimonies, in talking about each of her companions? And what details she herself was able to share! Her meeting in Paris with the Mother Prioress, the moving spectacle they had witnessed together, the last words they had exchanged! As for her own adventures since that time, they were undoubtedly what she spoke about least.

The fall of Robespierre had had no effect on the English Benedictine Nuns detained at the Visitation other than to remove the threat of death from them; otherwise, the months passed without any improvement in their condition. They could only obtain bread by paying for it, and even then they were not able to procure but an insufficient quantity of it, and of poor quality. When winter came, they had no warm clothes and no fire; at night, they had to content themselves with a thin woolen blanket. However, from December 23, 1794 (was it as a result of complaints from the English government?), they were granted an allowance of 40 sols[8] per day per person, which was paid to them until March 23, 1795.[9]

---

8 [TN] 40 sols (or sous) was 2 livres (pounds). In the late 18th century, a single livre could represent a significant portion of a daily wage for a laborer.

9 On 25 Germinal Year III (April 14, 1795), the Convention, based on the report of Jard-Panvilliers, issued the following decree (Mon., v. xxiv, p. 223): "The National Convention, having heard the report of the Committee of Public Safety, decrees: Art. I[st]. English nuns from various communities established in France, whose property has been seized pursuant to the decrees of the National Convention, shall receive, from the funds made available to the Public Relief Commission, a stipend of 40 sols per day for each individual, until a final ruling has been made concerning the seizure of their property." We can see from what happened to the Benedictines that they actually benefited from this decree four months before it became official. The same was true elsewhere as in Compiègne: the district advanced the necessary sums to be reimbursed by the State; this was also the case in

On that date, their allowance was withdrawn, but they were allowed to bring money from England by means of Hamburg. The mayor of Compiègne secretly advised them to request passports from Paris and forwarded their petition himself. It was promptly and completely successful, and ten days later, the district of Compiègne informed them that they were free.

It was undoubtedly at this moment that Sister Marie of the Incarnation was allowed to join them. How eager she must have been to meet with these Nuns, in the vicinity where her Sisters of Carmel had resided for several weeks; who were familiar with the same sufferings and could give her some idea of what they were like; who had received their adieus from afar, and witnessed their departure! She saw them and, according to an English account, spared no effort to help them in every way possible. For eighteen months, the Benedictines had been deprived of hearing Mass: Sister Marie of the Incarnation provided them with everything they needed, and Reverend James Higginson celebrated Mass in the prison.

Declared free, the English Benedictines could not consider staying in France: France had ceased to be a land of hospitality. On the other hand, England, which had been so widely open to French priests and even religious, was relaxing, if only out of a sense of logical consistency, its centuries-old harshness towards its Catholic citizens. English Monks, and Nuns also, who had taken refuge in Belgium had already returned to their homeland, and even with the personal help of King George III: the Benedictine Nuns hastened to follow their example. There were seventeen of them. The preparations being finished, towards the end of April, the abbess and three of the oldest Nuns left by stagecoach; On the 24th, the thirteen other Nuns left Compiègne upon carriages, no doubt for reasons of economy. They all met up in Calais, where they embarked upon a Danish ship and arrived in Dover on the evening of May 2, 1795. Dom Higginson and the Honorable Thomas Roper accompanied them. Such was their poverty that they

---

Gravelines, as can be seen in Art. 2 of the decree of April 14.

had had to continue wearing the garments of the Carmelites that were given to them by the mayor of Compiègne; they were still wearing them when they disembarked in England.[10]

On May 6, 1795, the Revolutionary Tribunal of Paris, which was reorganized on 8 Nivôse Year III,[11] after having held 39 sessions, and hearing 196 prosecution witnesses and 223 defense witnesses (for a total of 419) granted complete freedom to both the defendants and their defenders, guaranteed all the rights and legal prerogatives to those men who had so long trampled on them, and condemned to death Fouquier-Tinville, three former judges of the Revolutionary Tribunal, including Scellier, six former jurors, and six individuals who had been almost spontaneous accomplices to their crimes.[12]

The *Moniteur*, which was now no longer silent as it was during the Reign of Terror, enlightens us on the particular attitude of Scellier, the man from Compiègne who presided over the hearing at which the Carmelites were condemned: "The president (Agier) read out the sentence of condemnation; the greater part of the condemned expressed their dissatisfaction in the most scandalous manner...Scellier had shown himself to be the most seditious and indecent: throughout the entire proceeding, he had pretended to have great gentleness and moderation; but at the fatal moment, he displayed all the fury of a proud and wicked character. When the President pronounced these words: "The verdict of the jury is that Scellier is an accomplice and that he acted with

10 After a three week stay in London, they went to Woolton, near Liverpool, and in 1807 to Salford House, near Evesham. In 1838, they moved to Stanbrook, near Worcester. It was there that the ecclesiastical tribunal received their depositions. The abbess, now deceased, was Dame Gertrude Laure d'Aurillac Dubois, originally from Berlin, from a French family that had taken refuge there after the revocation of the Edict of Nantes; she died on October 19, 1897.

11 [TN] December 28, 1794

12 Fouquier-Tinville unanimously on the facts and intent; Scellier, Foucault, and Garnier-Launay by a majority of more or less votes on intent. Mon. v. xxiv, p. 401.

malicious intent," Scellier replied, "They have lied." Scellier was wearing a hat: a gendarme tried to remove it, and Scellier threw it out the window in a fit of rage...Scellier, whose physical strength had been almost sapped by a continual state of illness, wanted to recite a few sentences accompanied by oratorical gestures. Despair and his weakness stifled his voice; he fell back onto his bench, exhausted and still full of anger. At every moment, he uttered new insults. "Your turn will f…ing come, and it won't be long." This state of fury was shared by all of his companions."[13]

The next day, at eleven o'clock in the morning, the sixteen condemned men were sent on three carts to the *Place de Grève*: an immense multitude covered them with jeers and curses. Fouquier-Tinville was executed last; the people demanded his head. The executioner seized it by the hair and held it up for the crowd to see.

13 Mon., loc. cit. p, 402.

CHAPTER XVI

Spanning a Century

(1794-1894)

Even before the Consulate and during the entire time of the Empire, we see that the female Congregations gradually reformed themselves in the towns where they had lived before the Revolution: between 1798 and 1810, twenty-one Carmelite monasteries were reestablished. In Compiègne, no attempt was made to rebuild. How could this be surprising? The manpower was missing. Of the three Nuns that Providence seemed to have spared, Madame Legros had died; Madame Philippe was seriously ill; and Madame Jourdain was very old and perhaps did not have the requisite abilities. On the other hand, with every monastery of Carmel reduced by death, age, or illness, how could one think of recruiting new members to found a new one? There was no shortage of valiant and pious souls in Compiègne who would have liked to revive such a glorious house: but, were there not also some charitable considerations to be given to the surviving members of the municipal and revolutionary committees and their families?

It is certain that in 1814, the Duchess of Angoulême, faithful to these great memories, considered re-establishing the convent; and that in 1834, Duke Mathieu de Montmorency wanted to buy back the old buildings: but these attempts came to nothing.

In 1834, either on her own initiative or at the urging of Abbé Auger, curé of the parish of Saint-Antoine, Mother Camille de Soyecourt came to install several Nuns lent from the convents of Pontoise, Troyes, and Reims in Compiègne. It was in the house at 9 *Rue Saint-Antoine* (formerly *Rue de Dampierre*) where, for twenty-two months, the Mother Prioress and several of her companions had lived. As if consecrated by their long stay that they had there, it was called "the place of the little martyrdom." A generous Christian woman from the city, Madame Garanger, rented the house for nine years. On March 25, 1835, the anniversary of the foundation of the first monastery, a council of ladies was established to raise funds. Perhaps in memory of the Confraternity of the Scapular that had been formed during the Revolution, another was organized to regulate vows and prayers. The curé provided an altar, a painting of the Annunciation (which was the name of the monastery), priestly vestments, and the necessary furnishings. The chapel was blessed on May 25, 1835; four Sisters, including Mother Camille de Soyecourt, attended the ceremony.

That same year, Abbé Auger published a short and concise leaflet, in which he quickly recounted the edifying annals of the monastery since its foundation. The inhabitants of Compiègne recognized in it many families from their town who, for a century and a half, had given the monastery Nuns and Prioresses distinguished by their spirit and piety. He devoted only a few pages to the servants of God who had been reaped by the scaffold: since, except for vague stories, what was really known at the time? He praised the zeal and charity of his fellow citizens; he praised their prudence no less, which confirms the observation we made above. Finally, he anticipated a common objection, which he had no doubt heard: would these Nuns not be a burden on the city and its inhabitants? "The Carmelites," he said, "provide for the maintenance of their monastery either through their personal fortune or through manual labor, according to the spirit of Saint Teresa. Once established, they are not a burden. Piety and gratitude at first establish them, and thereafter merely serve to support them."

Abbé Auger's personal involvement did not end there. The initial location on *Rue Saint-Antoine*, despite the memories it evoked, did not seem suitable: so he purchased (March 25, 1838) a more extensive property on 43 *Rue de la Porte-Paris* (the same property from which Bertier de Sauvigny had been taken on July 21, 1789), and the following year, on May 21, 1839, he enlarged it further with a new acquisition. However, despite the local sympathy that had greeted its re-establishment, the monastery languished, either because it lacked a Prioress who was a woman of initiative and authority, or because the Nuns, coming from different houses, were not imbued with the same spirit. Soon Abbé Auger transferred his acquisition to three Carmelite Nuns; they left only two Converse Sisters as guardians and resold the building on February 7, 1850.[1]

Sixteen years later, in 1866, a fresh attempt was made, and this time it was crowned with success. The monastery of Troyes was preparing to establish a new foundation in the Diocese. In agreement with Bp. Gignoux, the Bishop of Beauvais, the Bishop of Troyes allowed the group of Nuns to move to Compiègne. On September 3, 1866, the Prioress arrived there to supervise and organize the preparations for the new monastery.

At the end of *Rue Saint-Lazare,* there was a vast enclosure with buildings in ruins and almost uninhabitable. Thanks to the generosity of the Riant Family from Paris and a few families from Compiègne, this land was purchased; the Empress Eugénie wanted to ensure the future of the monastery through her generosity. The essential work was carried out: everything remained poor, almost inadequate, and temporary; but the enclosure was complete. It was decided to wait until later, when resources would allow, to build a monastery more in line with the prescriptions of Saint Teresa.[2] In a pastoral letter dated January 6, 1867, Bp. Gignoux, announcing the upcoming blessing of this Carmel, wrote: "If there was one town in our Diocese that ought to have been the first to revive the traditions of centuries past by bringing

1 Cf. Alex. Sorel, op. cit., pp. 78-79, n.

2 The first stone of the new buildings now inhabited by the Carmelites was laid and blessed by Bp. Gignoux on May 3, 1874; the installation took place on July 25, 1875. Ten years later (July 8, 1885), the first stone of the current chapel was laid; it lacks a portal.

back the daughters of Saint Teresa, it was indeed Compiègne. For it was Compiègne whose monastery of Carmelites dated back almost to the introduction of the reform of Carmel in France; Compiègne, which these holy Nuns had filled for a century and a half with the fragrance of their virtues; Compiègne, finally, which several of them made famous with their glorious martyrdom."

He recounted this martyrdom: "Seventy years have passed," he added, "and it is after an interruption of almost three quarters of a century that the monastery of the Carmelites of Compiègne will rise from its ruins...Come, then," he exclaimed, "pious Carmelites...Your holy companions, whom history has already named the martyrs of Compiègne, greet your arrival within these walls and pray for you from Heaven. Come, and revive those most pure virtues whose fragrance you will still find here, that regularity and that fervor which edified our ancestors. May your presence draw abundant blessings upon Compiègne and upon this Diocese!" It was indeed under the auspices of the glorious servants of God that a new group of Carmelites came to Compiègne to resume the tradition that had been violently broken. January 18th, the feast of the Chair of St. Peter in Rome, was chosen by the Bishop for the definitive installation of the Nuns, the blessing of the chapel, and the declaration of enclosure.

When the day arrived, after the votive Vespers of Saint Teresa was chanted at the Church of Saint-Jacques, and a sermon for the occasion was delivered by Father Le Rebours, canon of Paris and Superior of the Carmelites of the capital,[3] the procession was organized to go to the monastery. At the head walked the young girls from two boarding schools in the

3 Since then, curé of Sainte-Madeleine, in Paris. His grandfather, J.-B. Auguste, president of the Third Chamber of Inquiry at the Parliament of Paris, had been sentenced to death with his colleagues by the Revolutionary Tribunal on June 14, 1794: this was the first day that the remains of the victims of the *Place du Trône* were thrown into the Picpus pit, to be joined, a month later, with those of the Carmelites.

city, wrapped in their white veils; followed by the Children of Mary, the Associates of the Rosary, the Sisters of Compassion, the Ladies of St. Joseph, the Sisters of St. Aubin, and the Daughters of Charity. The Carmelites walked in the middle, carrying only lighted candles, preceded by the humble little wooden cross held by a Converse Sister. Behind them came the clergy and the Bishop, followed by ecclesiastics from neighboring villages, the Brothers of the Christian Schools, and an immense crowd, recollected and chanting the Litany of the Saints. Despite the season, the weather was pleasant, and, according to the account of the Prioress, from whom we borrow the salient details of this solemn day, "the sun, before descending below the horizon, cast its most brilliant rays of light on this religious scene...As for us, deeply moved..., we said to ourselves that our martyred sisters were undoubtedly hovering above us during this magnificent ceremony!"

This same sentiment was expressed to the Mother Prioress by a vicar from Saint-Jacques, who had witnessed the event: "Since 1867, that is to say for thirty years, I have forgotten many things, but the memory of your installation remains one of the fondest memories of my priestly life. The ceremony was beautiful, solemn, pious, and truly moving; the crowd was extraordinary, and immense, for all of Compiegne was there: high society, the bourgeoisie, and the people. And yet that is not what had struck me the most. What particularly and vividly caught my attention was the deep emotion that dominated the entire procession, the assistants, and the clergy. People were visibly reviving the past, thinking about the bad days, remembering what they had heard, and in these moments of veneration which you had ushered in, you obviously had played your part. But above all, everyone believed they were paying tribute to those Nuns who were no longer with us, and whom the Revolution had treated so cruelly. It had to be this way, for your dear martyrs had left behind the most magnificent memories in Compiègne through their virtues and heroic courage."[4]

The Carmel of 1866, the successor to the one of 1794, had the duty to safeguard the memory of its heroic mothers from the previous century. It did not fail to do so, and, as in many places, the anniversary of the tragic dates of the Revolution gave rise to religious commemorations. Likewise, with the approach of the 100th anniversary of July 17, 1794, the Reverend Mother Prioress and her companions, in agreement with their Superiors, thought it appropriate to solemnize it with special celebrations. Bp. Fuzet, then the Bishop of Beauvais, in a letter addressed to the Mother Prioress, authorized her to celebrate a triduum of prayers at the Carmel on July 15, 16, and 17. It was celebrated with great pomp and circumstance. All the Carmels in France took part, not only in union of prayer, but also by sending banners, richly embroidered flags, and decorations of all kinds.

Monsieur de Maindreville, curé of the parish of Saint-Antoine, spared neither his personal efforts, his purse, nor his care for the splendor of the ceremonies he presided over. Each day of the Triduum was marked by a discourse recalling the heroism of the victims and renewing sentiments of admiration for their sacrifice.[5]

These discourses, printed and sent out far and wide, reawakened memories which were fading. Cardinal Bourret, the Bishop of Rodez, expressed his surprise that a canonical inquiry into the beatification of the sixteen Carmelites had not yet been initiated, and spontaneously promised his personal

4 Abbé Darras, curé of Pont Sainte-Maxence, letter dated June 1897.

5 Cf. *Souvenir du premier centenaire du martyre des Carmélites de Compiègne, Discours prononcés au Carmel de Compiègne les 15, 16, 17 juillet 1894.* (Commemoration of the First Centenary of the Carmelite Martyrs of Compiègne. Speeches preached at the Carmel of Compiègne on July 15, 16, 17, 1894). Compiègne, 1894. The speakers during the *triduum* were Monsieur Lagueau, curé-archpriest of Notre-Dame de Noyon; Monsieur Blond, Vicar General of Beauvais, since deceased (June 3, 1899), the author of the remarkable **biography** of Mother Charlotte of the Resurrection (Aune Thouret); and Monsieur Moreau, Honorary Vicar General of Langres.

assistance. The Carmels responded eagerly and joyfully: while some had lost track of this glorious past, many others, in France and abroad, bore witness to the tradition they had preserved, recalled the memory of their oldest mothers, and enthusiastically joined in the desires of the Carmelite convent in Compiègne!

Nowhere perhaps, more than in England, did these desires meet with a more sympathetic response. The story of the Carmelites had been known there almost overnight after their martyrdom; the English Benedictines of Cambrai, returning from France, had brought it with them. As early as 1795, the Reverend Milner, then a priest in Winchester (in 1803, he would become Vicar Apostolic of the Midlands, a district that included central England), published an account of it in *Laity's Directory,* which for a long time was the only digest for English Catholics. One of the nuns of Cambrai who had also been detained at the Visitation gave an eyewitness account of the sufferings of her companions. This composition, along with that of Reverend Milner, propagated this tradition among English Catholics, and devotional books seized upon it as a glorious example to offer to the Faithful.

What else did we discover? These clothes belonging to the Carmelites, which the English Benedictines of Cambrai had been forced to wear and which, because of the torture of July 17, 1794, had become precious relics, were sent by the Superior of the Benedictines between 1795 and 1804 to the Carmel of Darlington, along with a letter authenticating them.[6] The

6 Here is the translation: "I have sent you a few small objects that belonged to the Carmelites: I am sorry I have nothing better to offer; it is because I have given almost everything away. The garments we were given were not those in which they were executed, but those they had worn beforehand, and had left in the prison where we ourselves were held. The townspeople ordered us to take off our garments and brought us those of the Carmelites. They were in a room opposite us. We saw them being led by guards to the door to leave for Paris. I had the pleasure of talking to them twice, not without great fear." (Letter from Madame Mary Blyde, Abbess of the Benedictines of Woolton – now in Stanbrook, Birminghamshire – to

Prioress of Compiègne requested a portion of them; this request was granted, and these precious objects, which were entrusted to Reverend Murnane (as no one wanted to send them by post), crossed the strait on May 2, 1895, that is to say, exactly one century after the Benedictine nuns of Cambrai had crossed the sea, wearing these same garments, to return to their homeland.

Exercising his right of initiative, which belonged to him as Bishop of the place where the sacrifice had taken place, Cardinal Richard, the Archbishop of Paris, opened the process on February 23, 1896. Less than seven years later, on December 16, 1902, Pope Leo XIII announced the introduction of their cause for beatification and declared the sixteen Carmelites as Venerable. How can we be surprised at the relatively rapid success of this cause and the favor it has met with? Where else, among a group of those condemned during the Terror, can one find a more wonderful unity in a supernatural desire for sacrifice, a fidelity more constant, a greater prudence and steadfastness, an equal zeal for a holy death, or such a simplicity in submitting to it? The horror of torture disappears in admiration for these victims.

The apostolic process, which began on June 22, 1903, was closed on January 27, 1904. Several supernatural interventions were canonically recorded: it does not seem rash to hope that our Holy Father, Pope Pius X, will show no less sympathy for the cause of the Carmelites than his illustrious predecessor.[7]

Mother Marie Bernard, Carmelite of Darlington). According to a letter from Mother Thérèse Élie of Jesus and Mary, of the Carmel of Darlington, to the Prioress of the Carmel of Compiègne, the "small objects" mentioned in the letter of Madame Mary Blyde consisted of: "1. a piece of fine white muslin; 2. another piece of muslin, slightly thicker and striped; 3. a piece of red and white colored cloth and two halves or quarters of sleeves of the same colored cloth with buttons, probably belonging to some prison corsage."

7 We recall that the beatification was proclaimed and that the Blessed were celebrated in a solemn triduum at Saint-Sulpice, the parish of the Prioress, on June 18, 19, and 20, 1906 (Editor's note).

In June 1795, a French Bishop exiled in England was preparing to return to France. A lady lamented to him the destruction of so many relics of the saints. "Relics?" interrupted the prelate, "we will make more of them." Indeed, from 1792 to 1800, how many Priests, Monks and Nuns, women and girls of the nobility, of the bourgeoisie and of the common people were persecuted and put to death for their faith! Many causes have already been initiated: the sixteen Carmelites of Compiègne, proclaimed Venerable, are leading the way, and others will undoubtedly follow.

Discover Our Other Books:

The 1955 Holy Week, Fr. Olivier Rioult – $10 (ebook), $13 (paperback)

Modernism in the Church, Charles Périn – $10 (ebook), $13 (paperback)

The Drama of the End of Times, Fr. Emmanuel André – $10 (ebook), $13 (paperback)

Christ in the Home, Fr. Raoul Plus – $19 (paperback)

A Catholic Introduction to Love and the Facts of Life, Fr. Noël Barbara –$14 (ebook), $21 (paperback)

Life of Blessed Noël Pinot, Msgr. Alexis Crosnier –$16 (ebook), $24 (paperback)

The Anti-Christian Conspiracy, Msgr. Henri Delassus –$25 per part (pre-release translation project)

www.ingramcontent.com/pod-product-compliance
Lightning Source LLC
LaVergne TN
LVHW010659110826
845149LV00014B/3160

* 9 7 8 1 9 6 7 6 9 7 0 2 1 *